Bird Inventories of Big Hole National Battlefield, Nez Perce National Historical Park, and Whitman Mission National Historic Site 2005

UPPER COLUMBIA BASIN NETWORK

UCBN

Upper Columbia Basin Network

I0415761

Natural Resource Report NPS/UCBN/NRR—2009/125

Rita Dixon
Idaho Conservation Data Center
Idaho Department of Fish and Game
600 S. Walnut Ave, P.O. Box 25
Boise, ID 83707

Lisa K. Garrett
National Park Service, Upper Columbia Basin Network
University of Idaho, Department of Fish and Wildlife
Moscow, ID 83844-1136

August 2009

U.S. Department of the Interior
National Park Service
Natural Resource Program Center
Fort Collins, Colorado

The National Park Service, Natural Resource Program Center publishes a range of reports that address natural resource topics of interest and applicability to a broad audience in the National Park Service and others in natural resource management, including scientists, conservation and environmental constituencies, and the public.

The Natural Resource Report Series is used to disseminate high-priority, current natural resource management information with managerial application. The series targets a general, diverse audience, and may contain NPS policy considerations or address sensitive issues of management applicability.

All manuscripts in the series receive the appropriate level of peer review to ensure that the information is scientifically credible, technically accurate, appropriately written for the intended audience, and designed and published in a professional manner. This report received informal peer review by subject-matter experts who were not directly involved in the collection, analysis, or reporting of the data. This report received formal peer review by subject-matter experts who were not directly involved in the collection, analysis, or reporting of the data, and whose background and expertise put them on par technically and scientifically with the authors of the information.

Views, statements, findings, conclusions, recommendations, and data in this report are those of the author(s) and do not necessarily reflect views and policies of the National Park Service, U.S. Department of the Interior. Mention of trade names or commercial products does not constitute endorsement or recommendation for use by the National Park Service.

This report is available from the Upper Columbia Basin Network website (http://www.nature.nps.gov/im/units/UCBN) and the Natural Resource Publications Management website (http://www.nature.nps.gov/publications/NRPM).

Please cite this publication as:

Dixon, R., and L. K. Garrett. 2009. Bird inventories of Big Hole National Battlefield, Nez Perce National Historic Park, and Whitman Mission National Historical Site 2005. Natural Resource Report NPS/UCBN/NRR—2009/125. National Park Service, Fort Collins, Colorado.

NPS 100155, August 2009

Contents

Contents (continued)

Contents (continued)

Figures

Tables

Tables (continued)

Executive Summary

The mission of the National Park Service is "to conserve unimpaired the natural and cultural resources and values of the national park system for the enjoyment of this and future generations" (National Park Service 1999). To uphold this goal, the Director of the NPS approved the Natural Resource Challenge to encourage national parks to focus on the preservation of the nation's natural heritage through science, natural resource inventories, and expanded resource monitoring (National Park Service 1999). Through the Challenge, 270 parks in the national park system were organized into 32 inventory and monitoring networks.

The Upper Columbia Basin Network (UCBN) has identified 14 priority park vital signs, indicators of ecosystem health, which represent a broad suite of ecological phenomena operating across multiple temporal and spatial scales. Our intent has been to develop a balanced and integrated suite of vital signs that meets the needs of current park management, and that also will accommodate unanticipated environmental conditions and management questions in the future.

The objectives of this study were (1) to compile a comprehensive species inventory of at least 90% of all breeding, transient, and migratory bird species that, under normal circumstances, occur within the management units of interest; (2) to provide relative abundance measures for each of the documented species; and (3) to provide the baseline information needed to develop a general monitoring strategy and design that can be implemented by the park once inventories have been completed, tailored to specific park threats and resource issues.

This study included eight Nez Perce National Historical Park sites: Buffalo Eddy, Spalding, Heart of the Monster, Lolo Trail and Lolo Pass / Musselshell Meadow, White Bird Battlefield, Old Chief Joseph Gravesite, Bear Paw Battlefield, and Big Hole National Battlefield. Four sites were in Idaho, two in Montana, one in Washington, and one in Oregon. Incidental to the study, Whitman Mission National Historical Site (WHMI) was visited once.

Acknowledgements

I thank Gerry Wright, Dan Foster, Lisa Garrett, and Leona Svancara for their leadership, direction, and support of this project. Pat Heglund and Dan Davis offered initial input on the study design. I am grateful to Collin Hughes for his insightful editing of this report. Tim Fischer of Big Hole National Battlefield and Arthur Currence of Bear Paw Battlefield assisted with logistical arrangements and were both generous and accommodating. I am grateful to the Nez Perce elders who graciously allowed me to join them in their memorials at the Milk River and Bear Paw Battlefield. They showed me a depth of human spirit that continues to both awe and humble me. I thank the community of Chinook, Montana, for its warmth and hospitality. I am grateful to Chris Paige and Tobin Kelley and Paul and Maxine Stahl for their hospitality during trips to Montana. Diane Mallickan provided a list of Nez Perce animal and plant names and recounted the story of the "wing dress" and its significance to Nez Perce culture. Doug Eury of Nez Perce National Historical Park and Jon James of Big Hole National Battlefield helped to facilitate these surveys. The staff at Big Hole National Battlefield provided assistance with bird and habitat surveys. But most of all, it is to the birds I sought, and the landscapes I wandered, that I owe my deepest appreciation.

Introduction

In 1998, Congress passed the National Parks Omnibus Management Act, which mandated a National Park program for the inventory and monitoring of biological resources within the system. The pragmatic purpose of this act is to compile and organize existing data and fill gaps through field investigations, so as to complement park management decisions. Priorities were based on the initial need for credible avian inventories in two targeted parks, Nez Perce National Historical Park (NEPE) and Big Hole National Battlefield (BIHO), which are currently administered as one unit. The rapidly changing landscapes of the twentieth century have raised the value and status of scientific inquiry. Today as never before, the need for species inventories continues, queued up in order to guide the development of diverse dialogues on the wild and our National Park system; these dialogues are based on an interdisciplinary synthesis among the disciplines of biology, history, ethnobiology, sociology, and philosophy. In other words, this avian study is part of the growing constructive program designed to conserve nature and serve the citizens of this nation.

Nez Perce National Historical Park was created to protect and provide interpretation sites that relate to early Nez Perce indigenous culture, the Lewis and Clark expedition, the fur trade, Christian missionaries, gold mining, the Nez Perce War of 1877, burgeoning logging, and other epochal activities and events that represent the complicated historicity of Nez Perce country and the nation's westward expansion (USDI 1997). Unlike traditional parks, this park is unique in that it includes sites in Washington, Oregon, Idaho, and Montana.

Nez Perce National Historical Park falls into three basic ecoregions: the shortgrass prairies of the Palouse Grasslands and Missouri Basin, the sagebrush steppe of the Columbia and Snake River Plateaus, and the conifer/alpine meadows of the Blue Mountains, the Salmon River Mountains, the basins and ranges of southwestern Montana, and the northern Rocky Mountains of Idaho and Montana (Bailey 1995).

Previous biological inventories conducted in the park are scant and some sites have not been studied at all. Avian inventories have been limited to a recent study by Monello and Wright (1998), which documented the species occurrence, diversity, and relative abundance of birds in areas of exotic weed infestations and on ecologically similar lands covered by native vegetation. Sites included in this study were Spalding, Heart of the Monster (E. Kamiah), White Bird Battlefield, and Big Hole National Battlefield. In an earlier study, Van Sickle (1987) documented the species composition, relative abundance, and distribution of vertebrates at Big Hole National Battlefield, which included an avian inventory. Pierce (1982) conducted a comprehensive floristic study of Big Hole National Battlefield, including an inventory of all vascular plants within the various plant communities, the nature of the vegetation at the time of the battle, and a management plan for vegetation on the Battlefield.

Within the park, management issues include concerns over the spread of exotic and noxious weeds—e.g., yellow starthistle (*Centaurea solstitialis*), scotch thistle (*Onopordum acanthium*), field bindweed (*Convolvulus arvensis*), poison hemlock (*Conium maculatum*), and others—and the preservation and interpretation of wildlife habitat, especially because of increasing commercialization and urbanization in surrounding areas. Federally listed threatened or endangered species or federal candidate species undoubtedly exist within the park boundaries.

This kindredness requires managers to consider potential mitigation to avoid impacts on special status species and/or wetlands that support such species.

Within this context, the objectives of this study were: (1) to compile a comprehensive species inventory of at least 90% of all breeding, transient, and migratory bird species that, under normal circumstances, occur within the management units of interest; (2) to provide relative abundance measures for each of the documented species; and (3) to provide the baseline information needed to develop a general monitoring strategy and design that can be implemented by the park once inventories have been completed, tailored to specific park threats and resource issues.

Study Areas

This study included eight Nez Perce National Historical Park sites: Buffalo Eddy, Spalding, Heart of the Monster, Lolo Trail and Lolo Pass/Musselshell Meadow, White Bird Battlefield, Old Chief Joseph Gravesite, Bear Paw Battlefield, and Big Hole National Battlefield. Four sites were in Idaho, two in Montana, one in Washington, and one in Oregon. Incidental to the study, Whitman Mission National Historical Site (WHMI) was visited once.

Buffalo Eddy
Buffalo Eddy (46°10′N, 116°56′W) is located approximately 20 miles (32 km) south of Lewiston, Idaho, in Asotin County, Washington, and lies within the sagebrush steppe ecoregion. This site consists of groups of rock outcroppings on the Snake River and encompasses an elevational gradient of roughly 175 m (from 230 m to 405 m).

Spalding
Spalding (46°26′N, 116°49′W) is located along U.S. Highway 95 approximately 10 miles (16.1 km) east of Lewiston, Nez Perce County, Idaho, at the confluence of the Clearwater River and Lapwai Creek. Much of the landscape is groomed exotics and includes an arboretum, which was established as part of the Spalding Memorial State Park in the 1930s. This low elevation site (roughly 244 m) lies within the Palouse Grasslands of the shortgrass prairie ecoregion.

Heart of the Monster
Heart of the Monster (46°12′N, 116°00′W) is located two miles upstream from a bridge across the Clearwater River in Kamiah, Idaho County, Idaho. This site is approximately 53 acres (21.5 ha) of NPS-owned land and encompasses an elevational gradient of roughly 7 m (from 349 m to 356 m). The site falls within the Palouse Grasslands of the shortgrass prairie ecoregion and is primarily grassland with a riparian corridor (dominated by black cottonwood, *Populus trichocarpa*) along the river and a wetland on the east side of Highway 12. A stand of black locust (*Robinia pseudo-acacia*) lies adjacent the wetland.

Lolo Trail and Lolo Pass/Musselshell Meadow
Lolo Trail is about 100 miles (161 km) long, and extends approximately from Weippe to beyond Lolo Pass (which is on the Idaho-Montana border), Clearwater and Idaho Counties, Idaho. From Lolo, Montana, to a few miles west of Lolo Pass, the trail closely follows U.S. Highway 12. It then follows the high mountain ridges north of the highway for more than 80 miles (129 km), eventually descending to the Weippe Prairie near Weippe, Idaho. This study included predetermined stops along the corridor between Musselshell Meadow (46°21′N, 115°44′W) and Glade Creek Camp (46°37′N, 114°34′W). There is a cooperative agreement between the Forest Service and the National Park Service regarding the management of this site. Musselshell Meadow is within the Palouse Grasslands of the shortgrass prairie ecoregion and the remainder of the Lolo Trail is within the conifer/alpine meadows ecoregion. This diverse site covers a wide range of forest types as well as camas and alpine meadows and encompasses an elevational gradient of roughly 979 m (from 1060 m to 2039 m).

White Bird Battlefield
White Bird Battlefield (45°47′N, 116°16′W) is located about 15 miles (24 km) south of Grangeville, Idaho, between U.S. Highway 95 and the old White Bird Grade, approximately 0.5 miles (0.8 km) from the town of White Bird, Idaho County, Idaho. This site is approximately

1,245 acres (504 ha) of sloping topography that retains much of the appearance it had in 1877. White Bird Battlefield is in the Palouse Grasslands of the shortgrass prairie ecoregion. The majority of the site is open grassland, but a riparian corridor dominated by black cottonwood follows White Bird Creek. There is a modified stock pond—Swartz Pond—within the study area boundary. Yellow starthistle has invaded the grasslands of the site and other exotics include black locust and various exotic grasses. The elevational gradient is roughly 309 m (from 519 m to 828 m).

Old Chief Joseph Gravesite
Old Chief Joseph Gravesite (45°20′N, 117°13′W) is located on the west side of Oregon Highway 82, just north of Wallowa Lake and one mile (0.6 km) south of Joseph, Wallowa County, Oregon. The site is a 5.1 acre (2.1 ha) cemetery in the conifer/alpine meadows ecoregion and is approximately 1344 m in elevation.

Bear Paw Battlefield
Bear Paw Battlefield (48°22′N, 109°12′W) is located about 16 miles (25.75 km) south of Chinook, Blaine County, Montana. The landscape at Bear Paw remains relatively undeveloped, but there is exotic and changing vegetation. Located within the Missouri Basin sites of the shortgrass prairie ecoregion, this 190-acre (77 ha) site consists of two communities: a small riparian zone and a grassland (primarily blue grama (*Bouteloua gracilis*), needle-and-thread (*Stipa* sp.), wild rose (*Rosa* sp.), willow (Salix spp.), and cattail (*Typha latifolia*)). Bear Paw encompasses an elevational gradient of roughly 19 m (from 893 m to 912 m).

Big Hole National Battlefield
Big Hole National Battlefield (45°38′N, 113°39′W) is located approximately 10 miles west of Wisdom, Montana, on Montana Highway 43, in Beaverhead County, Montana. This 655-acre (265-ha) unit is surrounded by ranching operations and the Beaverhead National Forest and maintains much of the character of 1877. Big Hole is in the conifer/alpine meadows ecoregion and is characterized by three different landforms: mountain slope, floodplain, and bench (Despain 1973). Pierce (1982) described three primary vegetation types on the slope: forest, which is dominated by Douglas-fir (*Pseudotsuga menziesii*) and lodgepole pine (*Pinus contorta*) with a small component of ponderosa pine (*Pinus ponderosa*); forest ravine, which is similar in composition to the floodplain; and sagebrush steppe, dominated by big sagebrush (*Artemisia tridentata*) and Idaho fescue (*Festuca idahoensis*) with several quaking aspen (*Populus tremuloides*) groves. Willow (*Salix* spp.), graminoid (tufted hairgrass *Deschampsia caespitosa*/sedge *Carex* spp.), and aquatic communities characterize the floodplain. The bench has two primary communities: grassland, which is dominated by Idaho fescue/bluebunch wheatgrass (*Elytrigia spicata*, previously *Agropyron spicatum*); and shrubland, which is dominated by big sagebrush/Idaho fescue (Mueggler and Stewart 1980). The elevational gradient is roughly 139 m (from 1869 m to 2008 m). For a more detailed description of the site, see Pierce (1982).

Whitman Mission National Historic Site
Whitman Mission National Historic Site (NHS) (46°02′N, 118°27′W) is located approximately seven miles (11.3 km) west of the city of Walla Walla, Walla Walla County, Washington. West of the Blue Mountains, this 98.15 acre (39.75 ha) historic site is on a portion of the original land settled by Marcus and Narcissa Whitman, Presbyterian missionaries, in 1836 and lies within the Palouse Grassland Ecoregion.

Methods

Sampling Strategy, Sampling Frame and Sample Selection

The overall sampling strategy for the park was designed to gain a comprehensive picture of the avian communities present at each of the study sites during the course of the year. I accounted for spatial factors by using a systematic sampling design (Ratti and Garton 1996) for the placement of point count stations. I established points at 250 m intervals along equally spaced transects (at least 500 m apart) throughout each site. Because each site varied in size, the number of point count stations varied among sites: three at Buffalo Eddy, six at Spalding, four at Heart of the Monster, 24 at White Bird Battlefield, one at Old Chief Joseph Gravesite, and 10 at Bear Paw Battlefield. The exception to this systematic sampling design was at Big Hole National Battlefield, where I was able to locate and subsequently use 10 (points 1-8, 11-12) of the 13 plots that had been established by Pierce (1982) in the three major landforms at Big Hole National Battlefield; and at Lolo Trail and Lolo Pass/Musselshell Meadow, where 16 predetermined points along the corridor had been identified for the study (Glade Creek Camp, DeVoto Memorial Grove, Powell Ranger Station, Snowbank Camp, Bear Oil and Roots, Indian Post Office Lake, Howard Camp, The Devil's Chair, The Smoking Place, Greensward Camp (Bald Mountain), Horse Sweat Pass, Weitas Meadows, Pete Forks, Salmon Trout Camp, Lewis and Clark Grove Camp, Musselshell Meadow).

The significance of the Lolo Trail points is that each of the points was a camp used by the Lewis and Clark expedition. Tourists will heavily use these camps during the upcoming Lewis and Clark bicentennial and the Park was particularly interested in obtaining baseline information for these specific points so that they could monitor any impacts from the increased traffic along this corridor. With the exception of Lolo Trail and Lolo Pass/Musselshell Meadow, (which I marked with a small (1.25-in) brass tag on the back of USFS signs), I marked each point count station with a 34-in rebar stake and a small (1.25-in) brass tag with the point number inscribed on it. In addition, when possible I recorded the UTM coordinates of each point count station using a Global Positioning System (GPS) receiver. To assure the accuracy of the distance between stations, I used a hip-chain to measure distance.

I accounted for temporal factors by sampling the sites during different seasons and by timing the surveys for the time of day when birds are most easily detected. I supplemented these efforts with additional area searches and tape playbacks to target rare species. I collected a suite of habitat variables at each point count station using a standardized protocol.

Point Counts

With few exceptions, I followed the general guidelines and procedures for point count censusing of birds by Ralph et al. (1993). I conducted unlimited-distance point counts from March 5, 1999 to December 21, 1999. Weather permitting, point counts were started within 0.5 hour after sunrise and completed before 11:00 (PST) for Idaho and Oregon sites and 12:00 (MST) for Montana sites. At each point count station, I recorded birds seen and/or heard during a 5-min period. I selected a 5-min sampling period based on recommendations of Ralph et al. (1995) and other researchers (Lynch 1995; Savard and Hooper 1995; Smith et al. 1995). These researchers found that a 5-min period was the most efficient sampling duration. I estimated the distance to each bird using a Bushnell Yardage Pro™ 400 laser rangefinder.

Area Searches

I supplemented point counts with area searches at selected point count stations. Area searches were conducted at Buffalo Eddy (point count station 3; 100 m radius), Spalding (point count stations 1-6; 100 m radius and point count stations 1, 3, 5; 200 m radius), Heart of the Monster (point count stations 1-4; 100 m radius), Lolo Trail and Lolo Pass/Musselshell Meadow (point count stations 1-16; 100 m radius), White Bird Battlefield (points 1, 11, 23; 100 m radius), and Old Chief Joseph Gravesite (point count station 1; 100 m radius). The intent of these searches was to detect and identify quiet birds. Area searches were not conducted at Bear Paw Battlefield or Big Hole National Battlefield, primarily because these sites were large and open and most birds were easily detected during point counts. I conducted a one-time extensive search of Whitman Mission National Historical Site. In addition, I conducted an area search at Colgate Licks National Recreation Trail. Area searches consisted of 20 minute point counts in which I systematically moved around in a predefined area. Ralph et al. (1993) recommended plot sizes of about 3 ha in forest or dense woodland, but suggested that larger areas of 10 ha or more could be used in more open habitats. In addition, these authors suggested that in very dense forest, smaller areas of 1-2 ha could be used. I used a 100 m radius plot for area searches, with the exception of a one-time 200 m radius area search at Spalding. I searched the same areas on each visit. Although the intensive nature of this method allows it to be carried out longer into the morning (Ralph et al. 1993), I attempted to restrict the searches until no later than five hours after dawn. I recorded the number of birds of each species seen, heard, or both seen and heard in the search area during this time. I recorded birds outside the search area separately, but concentrated on finding as many birds as possible within the plot. In addition to the systematic point counts and area searches, I recorded observations less formally the rest of the day.

Tape Playbacks

For specialized groups of birds, e.g., nocturnal owls, American three-toed woodpecker (*Picoides dorsalis*), and northern goshawk (*Accipiter gentilis*), I used tape playbacks in conjunction with point counts and area searches. The tape playbacks were only used at key times of the year for those species that are not easily detected during point counts. I followed the general guidelines and procedures for tape playbacks in the Payette National Forest Protocol for Broadcast Vocalizations (Payette National Forest 1993). Generally, the procedure involved broadcasting a sequence of calls and/or drums (e.g., American three-toed woodpecker) in a random direction (obtained from second-hand on watch) using a Johnny Stewart™ game caller. During the 30-sec pause after the first sequence, the game caller was rotated 120° for the second sequence, paused, then rotated another 120° for the final sequence of vocalizations. When the final sequence was complete, I remained at the calling station for 30 seconds before continuing to the next calling station. The following species were targeted using tape playbacks: northern goshawk, Boreal owl (*Aegolius funereus*), great gray owl (*Strix nebulosa*), flammulated owl (*Otus flammeolus*), and American three-toed woodpecker.

Breeding Status

During the course of the year, I recorded anecdotal observations of: active nests; birds carrying nesting material, food, or fecal sacs; distraction displays; courtship; copulation; and territorial singing or drumming on all species seen or heard during each visit to each site. With this information, I used methods similar to those employed at Monitoring Avian Productivity and Survivorship (MAPS) stations (DeSante et al. 2002) to determine the breeding (summer residency) status of all species at each site. I first recorded the Period Breeding Status (i.e., Confirmed, Probable, Observed) of each species encountered during each period (visit) at each site. I recorded the highest hierarchical period breeding status detected for each species that

6

period. As defined by DeSante et al. (2002), I used the following hierarchical criteria to designate Period Breeding Status:

Confirmed—current year's nest found in the study area with eggs or young, in the process of being built, or already depredated or abandoned; adult seen gathering or carrying nesting material to a likely nest site in the study area; adult seen carrying food or fecal sac to or from a likely nest site in the study area; distraction display or injury feigning by an adult bird; a young bird incapable of sustained flight (a "local") in the study area or very young (stub-tailed) fledglings found being fed by parents in the study area.

Probable—copulation or courtship observed of a species within its breeding range; other territorial behavior observed in the study area; territorial song or drumming heard.

Observed—bird encountered (seen or heard) in the study area but with no territorial behavior; bird encountered flying over the study area.

At the end of the year, I reviewed the period status codes and entered the apparent yearly breeding status of each species using one of the following six categories defined by DeSante et al. (2002):

Breeder (B): Summer resident—any species within its normal breeding range that was confirmed or determined to be a breeder or summer resident within the site (i.e., at least one individual was determined to reside at least partly within the site boundary during the breeding season of the year under consideration).

Likely Breeder (L): Probable summer resident—a species within its normal breeding range that was suspected to be a breeder or summer resident but was encountered somewhat infrequently during the breeding season of the year under consideration.

Transient (T): A species that breeds in the general area of the site (perhaps even less than a kilometer away), but, because of habitat, altitude, or patchy distribution, does not breed at the site.

Migrant (M): The site does not lie within the breeding range of the species, and the species did not reside at the site during the breeding season. Migrant species may pass through the site on migration, or reside through the winter.

Habitat Assessment
I followed the general guidelines and procedures for habitat assessment as outlined by Ralph et al. (1993). That is, I first established a releve (i.e., a variable radius plot) centered on a point count station. I accomplished this by walking around the point for about 5-10 minutes, or until I stopped adding new species, whichever was less. The distance from the stopping point, or the outermost boundary or vegetation that I could see from the point center, became the radius of the plot and was treated as the boundary for estimating relative abundance. The size of the plot varied from 30 m to 50 m, depending on the homogeneity of the vegetation composition and the density of the vegetation.

I determined the number of major vegetation layers within each releve by their dominant growth form: tree layer (T), shrub layer (S), herb (H) layer, and ground cover (moss and lichen) layer

(G). I used the following height classes for each stratum: the tree layer included any plants taller than 5 m; the shrub layer included woody plants from 0.5-5 m in height; the herb layer included any plants less than 0.5 m tall; and the moss/lichen layer included those plants less than 0.1 m high.

I determined the average height of each major layer present and the dominant plant species. In addition, I also recorded the maximum and minimum diameter at breast height (dbh) of canopy trees and the total percent cover value of each layer. I determined the relative importance of each species in each layer present, which was expressed as percent cover.

I recorded the following location and site data on a standardized data form created by Ralph et al. (1993): state or province, region, UTM coordinates, elevation (m), slope aspect to the nearest degree (with a compass), percent slope (with a clinometer), presence (+) or absence (-) of water within the releve, and plot radius (distance from the center to the edge of the releve). I also recorded the following vegetation structure and composition data: total cover of each of the four layers, according to the Braun-Blanquet (Mueller-Dombois and Ellenberg 1974) Cover Abundance Scale, which is: 5 = >75% cover; 4 = 50-75% cover; 3 = 25-50% cover; 2 = 5-25% cover; 1 = numerous, but less than 5% cover, or scattered, with cover up to 5%; + = few, with small cover; and r = rare, solitary with small cover; average height of the lower and upper bounds of each of the four layers, to the nearest decimeter (0.1 m); species with the greatest cover (foliage or crown cover) within each layer's boundary; for each layer where trees were present, the diameter at breast height (dbh) to the nearest centimeter of the largest tree in the layer and also for the smallest trees; and species of trees used for minimum and maximum dbh measurements. I also recorded the number of sublayers visible in each primary layer: "1" if the layer was uniform and "2" or more if more than a single layer was divided into sublayers.

For layers where sublayers were recognized, I recorded the sublayers with a letter designating the primary layer, followed by a number (e.g., T1, T2, T3, S1, etc.), which indicated the sublayers by decreasing heights. I recorded cover, as described above, using the Braun-Blanquet method. Finally, I recorded the species' name for each plant species that made up at least 10% of the cover.

Data Anyalysis and Evaluation

Using a combination of information obtained from point counts, area searches, tape playbacks, and field notes, I compiled a list of all bird species encountered over the course of the year at each site. I used a quantitative approach to estimating abundance and summarized these numerical estimates into abundance categories. Specifically, I expressed relative abundance as percent of total. That is, the total number of contacts (from unlimited-distance point counts) with a given species was divided by the total number of contacts for all species across all visits by site. From these results, I assigned each species one of four abundance scores, based on the following criteria. The least abundant 20% of species were scored 1 (rare), while the most abundant 20% were scored 4 (abundant). The remaining 60% of species was divided in half based on abundance, and assigned to categories 2 (uncommon) and 3 (common).

I created a subset of point count data limited to the breeding season (May 20, 1999 to July 26, 1999) to estimate density. Only birds observed within a 100 m radius from the center of the point count station were included in this analysis. Limiting the density estimation to the breeding season is justified in that many birds are not singing outside of the breeding season and consequently, the analysis might underestimate the actual density of certain species. I used

Program VCPS (Copyright, E. O. Garton), which incorporates the optimum nonparametric estimation of population density (ordered distance method; Patil et al. 1982), to estimate point and confidence intervals of density (birds/ha).

I used detections from point counts, area searches, and incidental sightings to assess breeding status of each species.

Results

Point Counts and Area Searches
Of the 164 species detected by point counts and area searches during the study period (Appendix; scientific names therein), 43 were detected at Buffalo Eddy (Table 1), 69 at Spalding (Table 2), 64 at Heart of the Monster (Table 3), 66 at Lolo Trail and Lolo Pass / Musselshell Meadow (Table 4), 84 at White Bird Battlefield (Table 5), 59 at Old Chief Joseph Gravesite (Table 6), 53 at Bear Paw Battlefield (Table 7), and 83 at Big Hole National Battlefield (Table 8). White Bird Battlefield and Big Hole National Battlefield contained the highest species richness among the eight sites sampled. Each of these sites contains diverse habitats, which includes riparian areas in each. These sites are also large compared to the other sites sampled. Buffalo Eddy contained the lowest species richness, which is likely due to the relatively homogeneous nature of the habitats, but may also be an artifact of its small size. Each of Tables 1 through 8 includes: abundance scores for each species; birds/count period, density (birds/ha), 90% CI, and total number for point count data truncated at 100 m during the breeding season (May 20, 1999 to July 26, 1999); total number and relative abundance based on untruncated point count data for the entire year; and breeding status.

Tape Playbacks
None of the five targeted species—northern goshawk, Boreal owl, great gray owl, flammulated owl, American three-toed woodpecker—were detected during tape playbacks. However, the American three-toed woodpecker was detected during a point count at Pete Forks along the Lolo Trail. I heard young begging during the count and subsequently located an active nest where I observed an adult female feeding one male and one female nestling young, which were near fledging. The nest was approximately 130 meters below the road at Pete Forks in a 30 cm dbh lodgepole pine snag.

Habitat Assessment
Plant species present at each site are summarized in Tables 10-17. Based on plant species composition, I assigned each point to the most appropriate ecological system (Comer et al. 2003; NatureServe 2003) (Table 18). I added descriptive modifiers to some of the systems when I could not find one that fit the plant species composition at the site. In addition, NatureServe's (2003) descriptions of ecological systems did not include disturbed or developed categories. In those cases, I attempted to best describe the point.

Special Status Species
The following comments apply to those species that warrant management attention because of the concern over their current conservation status.

Horned Grebe: Recorded only at Old Chief Joseph Gravesite as a migrant, breeding populations of this species are listed by the state of Oregon as a Sensitive Species in the peripheral or naturally rare category. This species' long contracting breeding range and negative trends, based on North American Breeding Bird Survey (BBS) and Christmas Bird Count data, most likely indicate that the few measures taken on its behalf in North America have exacted little positive effect (Stedman 2000). Within North America, the degradation of breeding sites results primarily from agricultural activities, such as the mowing of lacustrine vegetation in dry years and the eutrophication of aquatic sites from fertilizer and pesticide build-ups (Stedman 2000). In addition, grebes abandon lakes where shorelines contain many summer homes and where people recreate on the water during the summer months (Stedman 2000).

American White Pelican: Recorded as a migrant at Bear Paw Battlefield, the American white pelican is listed as a Species of Concern by the state of Montana (Montana Natural Heritage Program 2004). Until the early 1970s, combinations of changing water levels and human disturbance threatened the continental population of white pelicans (Evans and Knopf 1993). Since then, the population has recovered and appears to have recently stabilized, but the species remains potentially vulnerable to habitat degradation and disturbance (Evans and Knopf 1993). Most management concerns relate to breeding colonies. Protection of breeding colonies from human disturbance and protection of nesting and foraging habitat from widespread permanent flooding or drainage remain the primary management concerns (Evans and Knopf 1993). Although not recorded at any of the Idaho NEPE sites, an emerging and challenging conservation issue in Idaho is the conflict between piscivorous pelicans and special status native fish species.

Bald Eagle: Recorded as a migrant at White Bird Battlefield, Bear Paw Battlefield, and Big Hole National Battlefield, the bald eagle is listed as Threatened by the U.S. Fish and Wildlife Service (USFWS) in the lower 48 States. Endangered-species protection prohibits the "take" of bald eagles and also requires federal agencies to consider the impact of their actions on this species. Most management actions regarding the bald eagle have been directed toward the protection of nests and communal roosts (see Buehler 2000). Because the bald eagle does not appear to nest within any of the management sites inventoried in this study, management for this species within the Park should focus on the winter needs of bald eagles. Winter habitat suitability for bald eagles is defined by food availability, the presence of roost sites that provide protection from inclement weather, and the absence of human disturbance (Buehler 2000). Although not recorded at Spalding during any of the visits in 1999, bald eagles winter along the Clearwater River and the larger diameter ponderosa pine trees at Spalding offer potential roosts and perches for this species.

Swainson's Hawk: Recorded as a transient at Old Chief Joseph Gravesite, the Swainson's hawk has so reduced in numbers or distribution throughout its range that it is considered to be declining in Utah, Nevada, and Oregon (England et al. 1997). Although there is currently no federal status under the Endangered Species Act regarding this species, the Swainson's hawk is listed as an Oregon Sensitive Species in the Vulnerable Category, a Species of Special Concern in Utah, Nevada, and Washington, and Threatened in California (Littlefield et al. 1984; Herron et al. 1985; Harlow and Bloom 1989). Swainson's hawks commonly breed in areas of intensive agriculture; alfalfa fields and other hay fields seem particularly well suited to this species (England et al. 1997). On both the breeding and wintering grounds, conversion of native habitat to woody perennial crops and urban development eliminates habitat for Swainson's hawks (England et al. 1997). A preferred management technique is to provide tree plantings in areas where nest sites are limiting (Fitzner 1980).

Ferruginous Hawk: Documented as a confirmed breeder at Bear Paw Battlefield, the ferruginous hawk's population numbers have been on the rise at an average annual rate of 3.4% based on the North American Breeding Bird Survey data from 1966-1999. Despite this increase, this species is still recognized as a Species of Concern in Montana (Montana Natural Heritage Program 2004) and has seen many local declines (Bachand 2001). To maintain current population numbers, management measures should be directed toward enhancing nest substrates, maintaining prey populations, and mitigating development impacts from mining, pipeline construction, and urbanization (Suter and Jones 1980; White and Thurow 1985; Olendorff 1993).

In addition, wildland protection or an agricultural production system largely based on ranching—if maintained in substantial portions of both the breeding and wintering ranges—are consistent with ferruginous hawk conservation (Bechard and Schmutz 1995). Population declines have largely resulted from the effects of cultivation, grazing, poisoning and controlling small mammals, mining, and fire in nesting habitats, with cultivation being the most serious (Olendorff 1993).

Golden Eagle: Recorded as a transient at Buffalo Eddy, the golden eagle is a State Candidate Species in Washington, which means that it is under review for possible listing as State Endangered, Threatened, or Sensitive.

Franklin's Gull: Recorded only at Bear Paw Battlefield as a migrant, the Franklin's gull is listed as a Montana Animal Species of Concern (Montana Natural Heritage Program 2004). This gull is sensitive to human disturbance early in the breeding cycle and will entirely desert a colony site with excessive exposure to humans (Guay 1968). Nesting habitat degradation occurs as a result of the draining of marshes or intentional drawdown for management of duck-nesting habitat (DuMont 1940; Littlefield and Thompson 1981). The key management technique for Franklin's gulls is to maintain suitable water levels in large marshes (Burger and Gochfeld 1994). This gull deserts its breeding colonies from mid- to late July and wanders widely in all directions over large prairie regions (Burger 1972). In contrast, spring migration is more direct with less lingering en route to breeding colonies (Burger and Gochfeld 1994).

American Three-toed Woodpecker: Documented as a confirmed breeder at Lolo Trail and Lolo Pass/Musselshell Meadow, the American three-toed woodpecker was recently identified as a Species of Greatest Conservation Need in Idaho (Idaho Comprehensive Wildlife Conservation Strategy Draft SGCN list, January 2005) and is currently a U.S. Forest Service (USFS Region 4) Sensitive Species. This species' association with spatially unpredictable disturbance and its large home range size make it sensitive to timber harvesting and forest fragmentation, both which ultimately reduce food availability and have contributed to population declines (Leonard 2001). In addition, owing to their strong preference for bark beetles, American three-toed woodpecker populations are directly and negatively affected by pest management operations that target beetle host trees (e.g., lodgepole pine or spruce) (Leonard 2001). Fire suppression has also played a role in reducing habitat for American three-toed woodpeckers, which, like salvage logging, effectively reduces or removes the dead and dying trees on which this species depends (Leonard 2001). But more specifically, the alteration of natural fire intensity has likely resulted in population declines of this species (Hutto 1995).

Sprague's Pipit: Documented as a confirmed breeder at Bear Paw Battlefield, and locally abundant, the Sprague's pipit is considered a Species of Concern by the state of Montana (Montana Natural Heritage Program 2004) and recognized as a Sensitive Species by the U.S. Forest Service. Endemic to the North American grasslands and one of the least-known birds in North America, the Sprague's pipit has suffered dramatic declines in numbers throughout its range as prairie has disappeared via cultivation, overgrazing, and invasion by exotic plants (Samson and Knopf 1994; Robbins and Dale 1999). Based on North American Breeding Bird Survey data for the period between 1966 and 1999, the Sprague's pipit has declined in the western U.S. at an average annual rate of 7.4% (Bachand 2001). Studies designed to address the effects of Eurasian plant species on the densities of Sprague's pipits all showed a significantly greater abundance of Sprague's pipits in native prairie than in introduced vegetation (Wilson and Belcher 1989; Dale 1990, 1992, 1993; Hartley 1994; Davis et al. 1996; Madden 1996; Prescott

13

and Wagner 1996). Other issues affecting Sprague's pipits are the consequences of grazing and the encroachment of shrubs and trees throughout the wintering areas (Robbins and Dale 1999). Several factors contribute to the effects of grazing on pipit densities ranging from the frequency and duration of grazing to environmental conditions such as moisture, soil types, and plant species composition (Robbins and Dale 1999). Management for this species should include prescribed fire, which is important for controlling the encroachment of woody vegetation (Robbins and Dale 1999). Grazing can be used as an alternative to prescribed fire for preventing an overaccumulation of vegetation, especially in drier portions of the range (Robbins and Dale 1999). Moderate to heavy grazing in tallgrass and mesic mixed-grass prairie appears to have little impact and may even be beneficial to pipits (Kantrud and Kologiski 1982). However, studies in dry, sparsely vegetated mixed-grass prairie have demonstrated that grazing has a dramatic negative impact (Robbins and Dale 1999). Where haying is used to control vegetation, the timing of the harvest is critical to nest success; that is, cutting should be delayed until after the peak nesting period (Dale et al. 1997).

Brewer's Sparrow: Documented as a confirmed breeder at Big Hole National Battlefield (Table 8), the Brewer's sparrow is classified as a Montana Animal Species of Concern (Montana Natural Heritage Program 2004). Although not currently on any official state or federal list as threatened or endangered, recent surveys (1980s and 1990s) have shown this sagebrush obligate to be in significant decline rangewide—perhaps related to fundamental changes in shrubland ecosystems being brought about by agriculture, grazing, and the invasion of exotic plant species (Rotenberry et al. 1999). In addition, large-scale fragmentation and reduction in area of native shrublands has occurred throughout the Intermountain West (Braun et al. 1976), and may also be responsible for declines in Brewer's sparrows (Rotenberry 1998).

Little is known about the major aspects of this species' biology (Rotenberry et al. 1999). However, Brewer's sparrows are strongly associated with sagebrush shrublands that have abundant, scattered shrubs and short grass (Paige and Ritter 1999). They favor unburned sagebrush shrublands over burned sagebrush (Bock and Bock 1987), and in an Idaho study, high shrub cover and large patch size were important predictors of Brewer's sparrow occurrence (Knick and Rotenberry 1995). Brewer's sparrows are sensitive to sagebrush control, and thrive best where sagebrush is maintained in tall, clumped, and vigorous stands (Paige and Ritter 1999). The most critical conservation measure for breeding Brewer's sparrows is the protection and restoration of native shrublands and shrub-steppe habitats (Rotenberry 1998; Paige and Ritter 1999). Management recommendations include the removal of exotic annual plants that have become self-perpetuating (Rotenberry et al. 1999).

Grasshopper Sparrow: Recorded as transient at White Bird Battlefield, the grasshopper sparrow was recently identified as a Species of Greatest Conservation Need in Idaho (Idaho Comprehensive Wildlife Conservation Strategy Draft SGCN list, January 2005), is currently a Montana Animal Species of Concern (Montana Natural Heritage Program 2004), and in parts of the United States, some subspecies are both state and federally listed (Vickery 1996). The population decline of grasshopper sparrow and many grassland birds has been identified as a national and regional conservation priority (Knopf 1994; Vickery et al. in press). Although not documented at Bear Paw Battlefield in the present study, the grasshopper sparrow was recorded as rare at Bear Paw in 1997 (Monello and Wright 1998). Primary factors that have contributed to the long-term declines of grasshopper sparrow populations in North America include habitat loss, fragmentation, and degradation; e.g., the conversion of prairies and agricultural grasslands (Vickery 1996). In addition, extensive and intensive grazing in western North America has negatively impacted this species (Bock and Webb 1984). Three management techniques are recommended for this species: prescribed burning, grazing, and mowing; however, early-season mowing of hayfields and other agricultural lands is generally responsible for major nest failure (Vickery 1996). Deferred mowing on publicly owned lands would provide improved breeding opportunities for grasshopper sparrows and other grassland birds (Vickery 1996). A recent study showed that summer burns that correspond to the period of increased natural lightning strikes and wild fires could be beneficial for maintaining habitat and productivity (Shriver et al. 1996).

Baird's Sparrow: Found only at Bear Paw Battlefield in this study, and recorded as a likely breeder, the Baird's sparrow is a Species of Concern in Montana (Montana Natural Heritage Program 2004) and is also recognized as a Sensitive Species by the U.S. Forest Service and Bureau of Land Management. On May 21, 1999, the U.S. Fish and Wildlife Service issued a finding that the Baird's sparrow did not require Endangered Species Act protection. However, Service biologists concluded that the Service should continue to monitor the status of this species. A grassland specialist endemic to the northern Great Plains, the grasshopper sparrow has suffered population declines due to the conversion of native prairie to cropland and exotic vegetation, invasion of native grasslands by exotic plant species, proliferation of shrubs due to fire suppression in moist portions of Baird's sparrow distribution, and poor range management of some remaining tracts (Lane 1968; Owens and Myres 1973; Stewart 1975; Goossen et al. 1993; Green et al. 2002). Management for Baird's sparrow habitat should be directed toward protecting native prairie preserves (Green et al. 2002). In addition, in North Dakota, controlled burning appeared to be an effective management tool (Green et al. 2002).

Discussion

The avian communities of Nez Perce National Historical Park are as rich and as varied as the landscapes they occupy. The Park serves as a permanent home to many species, a summer breeding area for others, a place to rest and refuel for long-distance migrants, and a place for some species, such as the American tree sparrow to spend the winter. The Park is home to common species, such as the American robin, as well as some of the rarest, such as the American three-toed woodpecker. Some park sites are developed, whereas others, such as the Lolo Trail remain mostly wild. Bear Paw Battlefield stands as a remnant of what used to be a more extensive prairie system. Nevertheless, this remnant prairie site supports such rare species as the ferruginous hawk, Baird's sparrow, Sprague's pipit, long-billed curlew, and others.

Buffalo Eddy

For such a small site, and homogeneous nature, Buffalo Eddy nevertheless provides habitat for a diverse species assemblage. The steep and rocky slopes provide breeding habitat for rock and canyon wrens, American kestrels, and violet-green swallows. The Snake River provides habitat for great blue herons, belted kingfishers, and common mergansers. The hackberry draws provide nesting habitat for species such as the Lazuli bunting, Bullock's oriole, yellow-breasted chat, and spotted towhee; foraging corridors for the Cooper's hawk; cover for the western screech-owl; important forage and cover for migrants such as the black-capped chickadee, golden-crowned and ruby-crowned kinglet, yellow-rumped and MacGillivray's warbler, and dark-eyed junco. Powerline poles that cross through the site provide nest platforms for western kingbirds. Open country species that regularly inhabit this site include: golden eagle, common nighthawk, northern harrier, and red-tailed hawk. Chukars were common at this site; gray partridge and California quail were present, but were less common than the chukar. In 2000, a pair of Peregrine falcons occupied a ledge at Asotin Cliffs on the Snake River, but in the 1990s, a pair had nested at Ackerman Bar, which is just downstream from Buffalo Eddy. A species not detected in the present study, but one that I would have expected to find, is the prairie falcon. This area of the Snake River contains appropriate habitat and it is likely that this species occurs here in low densities.

Spalding

Species recorded by Monello and Wright (1998), but not detected in the present study at Spalding include: bank swallow (*Riparia riparia*), golden eagle, and common grackle (*Quiscalus quiscula*). Of these three species, the most surprising is the common grackle. This species is peripheral to Idaho and only breeds in the southeastern part of the state. However, it has been previously documented as transient in this latilong (Stephens and Sturts 1998).

An additional 53 species were added to Spalding from the present study. One of the more interesting species encountered at Spalding was the yellow-breasted chat. This species is typically found in dry areas near water and shrub cover, which exist at the edge of the site boundary to the east. Another interesting species encountered is the Bewick's wren. Stephens and Sturts (1998) record this species as wintering in this latilong, but it was documented in the present study as a breeder. This species seems to be expanding its range in Idaho. Spalding is a mix of habitats and Lapwai Creek flows through the site. The creek provides habitat for common merganser, great blue heron, Canada goose, wood duck, mallard, spotted sandpiper, Wilson's snipe, belted kingfisher, and yellow warbler, among others. The Clearwater River is used by both California and ring-billed gulls. The "boom" grounds to the east of the arboretum provide dense

17

cover for mixed-species flocks of migrants and wintering species such as brown creeper, black-capped chickadee, and white-crowned sparrow. The arboretum provides roost sites for great horned owls, and barn owls roost in the cottonwood and willow corridor adjacent to the river.

Heart of the Monster

Species recorded by Monello and Wright (1998), but not detected in the present study at Heart of the Monster include: varied thrush, bank swallow, common grackle, ring-billed gull, and fox sparrow. Varied thrush is interesting because this species is usually associated with conifer forests. However, it was likely migrating through. Both bank swallow and common grackle were also detected by Monello and Wright (1998) at Spalding, but I did not record them at any of the sites I visited. Ring-billed gulls frequent the Clearwater River and so would be expected at this site. Fox sparrow is another species that was likely migrating through.

An additional 53 species were detected in the present study. The slough that occurs between the Clearwater River and the site proper provides habitat for a variety of waterfowl and grebe species including: wood duck, mallard, northern shoveler, green-winged teal, and hooded merganser. Species such as the great blue heron, Canada goose, ring-necked duck, bufflehead, common goldeneye, common merganser, spotted sandpiper, belted kingfisher, and osprey frequent the Clearwater River, which provides breeding habitat for some and wintering habitat for others. There is a great blue heron rookery upstream and across the river from Heart of the Monster. The moist meadow at the south end of the site is prime habitat for the Wilson's snipe. The ephemeral wetland adjacent the RV Park opposite the highway from the main site offers habitat for migrating waterfowl and American coots, as well as habitat for red-winged blackbirds. The black cottonwood corridor along the river provides important breeding habitat for a wide variety of species including: downy woodpecker, northern flicker, red-eyed vireo, gray catbird, western wood-pewee, willow flycatcher, yellow warbler, Bullock's oriole, and black-headed grosbeak. Both mountain and western bluebirds occur at this site, but the mountain bluebird as a migrant only. Other key migrant species include: yellow-rumped warbler, black-capped chickadee, MacGillivray's warbler, white-crowned sparrow, and red-naped sapsucker. Both eastern and western kingbirds were documented at this site, the western as a confirmed breeder. A Cooper's hawk was detected hunting in the black locust stand across the highway and adjacent the wetland. However, this is a species poor stand that does not offer much in the way of habitat for species at this site.

Lolo Trail and Lolo Pass/Musselshell Meadow

Although this was the most extensive site in terms of coverage, the site was not accessible due to snow until past the ideal survey period for breeding birds. Therefore, it is likely that a number of species were not detected. That said, this site still had a diversity of species. One of the most notable species detected on the Lolo Trail was the American three-toed woodpecker. This species is typically found at higher elevations and is most likely to be found in lodgepole and/or Engelmann spruce forests. Another species that was only documented on the Lolo Trail was the spruce grouse. Chestnut-backed chickadees were detected only at Lewis and Clark Grove, which is western red cedar-hemlock forest. Key species associated with mountain hemlock forests included: brown creeper, fox sparrow, golden-crowned kinglet, mountain chickadee, pine siskin, varied thrush, white-crowned sparrow, winter wren, and yellow-rumped warbler. Most species encountered occurred across a range of habitats that included, in addition to the above: mixed conifer, lodgepole pine, spruce-fir, ponderosa pine, and riparian woodland and shrublands. The Lincoln's sparrow was an exception, and only occurred at two locations: Glade Creek and Weitas Meadow, which were subalpine-montane riparian shrubland and subalpine dry-mesic spruce-fir forest and woodland, respectively. One of the most species rich areas I found was in an alder thicket near Horse Sweat Pass and Spirit Revival Ridge. This thicket provided habitat for: Wilson's warbler, pine siskin, yellow-rumped warbler, Townsend's warbler, Nashville warbler, mountain chickadee, red-breasted nuthatch, rufous hummingbird, dark-eyed junco, and American robin. The Rufous hummingbirds were feeding on *Menziesia ferruginea* flowers.

White Bird Battlefield

Species recorded by Monello and Wright (1998), but not detected in the present study at White Bird Battlefield include: bank swallow, mountain bluebird, fox sparrow, short-eared owl, and vesper sparrow. There are highway cuts adjacent to the site, but they are mostly cut through basalt and don't offer the substrate that bank swallows need for nesting. I suspect the bank swallows observed by Monello and Wright (1998) were likely moving through the site, but not breeding. This is probably true of mountain bluebird and fox sparrow as well. White Bird could potentially support short-eared owls, but they were not observed in the present study. Vesper sparrow is considered a near obligate of sagebrush steppe in Wyoming, Nevada, and Idaho (Medin et al. 2000), and so it is not likely that White Bird would ever support a breeding population of this species.

In addition to the species detected by Monello and Wright (1998), 63 additional species were detected in the present study. Key grassland species included savannah sparrow, grasshopper sparrow, northern harrier, and western meadowlark. Other open country species included: turkey vulture, golden eagle, prairie falcon, Say's phoebe, western kingbird, and eastern kingbird. White Bird would likely support a greater diversity and higher density of grassland species if starthistle could be controlled. Both rock wrens and canyon wrens occupy the rocky cliffs of the battlefield as well as the basalt talus slopes above and below the highway. Two rail species were detected at White Bird: the sora and the Virginia rail. The sora was detected at Swartz Pond, but the Virginia rail was in a tiny patch of cattails near the entrance to the walking loop. Swartz Pond is one of the most important habitats on the Battlefield. This wetland provides habitat for migrating shorebirds and waterfowl, as well as breeding habitat for species such as red-winged and yellow-headed blackbirds. White Bird Creek supports red-eyed vireo, a species closely associated with riparian areas. The hackberry draws are important habitat for Lazuli buntings and yellow-breasted chats, as well as migrants such as the black-capped chickadee. Five exotic species were detected at White Bird: chukar, gray partridge, ring-necked pheasant, California quail, and European starling. The steep rocky slopes adjacent to the battlefield provide ideal habitat for chukars. Gray partridge were abundant, often in large expanses of starthistle. Bald eagles do not nest in this region, but are important winter visitors.

Old Chief Joseph Gravesite

Old Chief Joseph Gravesite, like Buffalo Eddy, is a small site. However, this site is at the mouth of Wallowa Lake, has an irrigation stream below the site, dense conifer forest opposite the site, and open country on the other side. Consequently, the species assemblage at this site was rich. Species detected from the site, but associated with Wallowa Lake include: horned grebe, Canada goose, mallard, common goldeneye, common merganser, and osprey. Key upland forest species included: sharp-shinned and Cooper's hawk, Vaux's swift, Clark's nutcracker, red-breasted nuthatch, brown creeper, golden-crowned kinglet, Townsend's solitaire, Swainson's thrush, yellow-rumped warbler, western tanager, red crossbill, and pine siskin. Because of the site's proximity to more open country, golden eagle, red-tailed hawks and American kestrels were detected from the site year-round, Swainson's hawk during the breeding season, and rough-legged hawk during the winter. The most interesting species detected at this site during the winter was the gray-crowned rosy-finch. Species associated with the riparian area include: belted kingfisher, red-naped sapsucker, warbling vireo, winter wren, and yellow and MacGillivray's warbler. Three swallow species—northern rough-winged, tree, and violet-green swallow—were detected during the study. Other species of note detected at the site include: great horned owl, calliope hummingbird, mountain bluebird, and Lazuli bunting.

Bear Paw Battlefield

Species recorded by Monello and Wright (1998), but not detected in the present study at Bear Paw include: Brewer's blackbird, lark sparrow (*Chondestes grammacus*), gadwall (*Anas strepera*), chipping sparrow, and grasshopper sparrow. I would have expected to find Brewer's blackbirds and grasshopper sparrows in the present study, but did not. I did observe lark sparrows in that region of Montana, but not at Bear Paw. Both Gadwall and chipping sparrows were most likely migrating.

An additional 35 species were recorded in the present study, which added several migratory species and wintering species. A pair of ferruginous hawks, (one light phase and one a rare dark morph), nested on the Davies' property beyond the corral and on top of a small knoll and produced five young. Other notable species at Bear Paw included the rare Baird's sparrow and Sprague's pipit, both recorded as breeders. The small ravines of common snowberry and pearhip rose provided habitat for clay-colored sparrows and short-eared owls. The clay-colored sparrow was one of the most abundant species at this site. Other grassland species included: vesper and savannah sparrow, willet, long-billed curlew, and western meadowlark. Two swallow species, cliff swallow and barn swallow occurred at the site. Of particular interest was a rock wren observed in October on the cutbank at the south end of the site. It was calling and I subsequently observed it. It was the only time I saw this species and I wonder if it was a dispersing juvenile. American white pelican, California gull, and Franklin's gull were observed en route to their breeding grounds, but did not actually stop at the site. Sandhill cranes were detected at the site, but apparently nested elsewhere. The coulee provided important habitat for many migrants including: American wigeon, northern shoveler, northern pintail, hairy woodpecker, black-capped chickadee, ruby-crowned kinglet, and Wilson's warbler. The coulee provided breeding habitat for mallard, yellow warbler, common yellowthroat, eastern kingbird, gray catbird, red-winged blackbird, and song sparrow. Bear Paw also provides wintering habitat for the bald eagle.

Big Hole National Battlefield

Species recorded by Monello and Wright (1998), but not detected in the present study at Big Hole include: common merganser (*Mergus merganser*), solitary sandpiper (*Tringa solitaria*), western flycatcher (*Empidonax difficilis*), ferruginous hawk, black-headed grosbeak, Wilson's warbler, and common yellowthroat. Big Hole is within the range of common merganser, and the Big Hole River could provide habitat. However, this species was not detected at any time during the course of the year. The solitary sandpiper does not breed in Montana, so it is likely that Monello and Wright (1998) encountered this species during migration. The western [Pacific-slope] flycatcher does not occur in Montana, but the cordilleran flycatcher (*E. occidentalis*) does. Neither of these species were recorded at Big Hole in this study. Monello and Wright (1998) reported scrub jay, but gave the scientific name *Perisoreus canadensis*, which is actually gray jay (and was recorded during this study). However, they also included an entry for gray jay with the same scientific name listed for scrub jay. Montana is not within the normal distribution of the [western] scrub-jay (*Aphelocoma californica*), nor is Big Hole typical habitat for this species.

Van Sickle (1987) recorded 24 additional species than encountered in the present study, most notably the northern goshawk, golden eagle, western screech-owl, MacGillivray's warbler, and spruce grouse. He, like Monello and Wright (1998), also recorded common merganser, solitary sandpiper, ferruginous hawk, and black-headed grosbeak. Of interest is that he recorded both Swainson's thrush and hermit thrush. Although these two species can overlap, the hermit thrush is more typically associated with higher elevation forests such as those at Big Hole. Van Sickle (1987) also recorded Williamson's sapsucker (*Sphyrapicus thyroideus*), which is typically associated with ponderosa pine forests.

Sixteen additional species—unique from Monello and Wright (1998) and Van Sickle (1987)—were encountered in the present study, which expands our knowledge of Big Hole's avifauna. Two winter residents of note recorded in this study were the American tree sparrow and the common redpoll. Other species of note include: bald eagle, rough-legged hawk, northern pygmy-owl, long-eared owl, Hammond's flycatcher, and Say's phoebe. But what is curious is that neither Monello and Wright (1998), nor Van Sickle (1987) recorded black-billed magpie. This species' presence is likely associated with adjacent ranch lands.

The willow flats along the river supported concentrations of veery, northern waterthrush, Lincoln's sparrow, and yellow warbler. The lodgepole pine forest on the mountain slope consisted of typical forest species including: Townsend's solitaire, hermit thrush, golden-crowned kinglet, Clark's nutcracker, and western tanager, among others. The sagebrush-steppe of the bench and mountain slope was represented by key sagebrush and/or grassland associated species such as the Brewer's sparrow, vesper sparrow, and savannah sparrow.

Whitman Mission

Species recorded by Monello and Wright (1998), but not detected in the present study at Whitman Mission include: ring-necked pheasant, Canada goose, bank swallow, common grackle, mallard, California quail, rock [pigeon] dove, American coot, red-tailed hawk, killdeer, black-capped chickadee, and warbling vireo. Because Whitman Mission was not originally one of the targeted sites, I only visited it once during the present study. So it is not surprising that these species were not detected. I did, however, detect an additional 13 species including: wood duck, sharp-shinned hawk, mourning dove, western wood-pewee, northern rough-winged and barn swallow, Bewick's and house wren, song sparrow, black-headed grosbeak, house finch, American goldfinch, and an unidentified hummingbird. Whitman Mission is in an agricultural area of eastern Washington, hence the bird community there is influenced by this. This site does support Swainson's hawks though, likely because of it's proximity to these same agricultural areas, which provide a prey base for this species.

Management Recommendations

Although each of the eight sites targeted in this study is unique, many of the sites share similar management issues. For example, the spread of exotic and noxious plants is paramount throughout the Park sites (U.S. Department of the Interior, National Park Service 1997). Monello and Wright (1998) conducted an inventory of exotic plants at four NPS units including five sites within the Nez Perce National Historical Park (Spalding, Heart of the Monster, White Bird Battlefield, Bear Paw Battlefield, Big Hole National Battlefield), and they found that, in proportion to its size, Spalding was the site most severely affected by exotic species and noxious weeds. However, each of the other sites inventoried had its own suite of exotics. Exotics such as yellow starthistle, scotch thistle, field bindweed, poison hemlock, and others rapidly outcompete existing vegetation. These species change the integrity of the environment and can affect bird communities in a number of ways. Tree species like black locust are not as suitable for nesting and foraging and therefore cannot support the number or diversity of birds that black cottonwood stands can support. Yellow starthistle invades and replaces native grass species that are important for both nesting and foraging. Thistle species replace native forbs that are important forage plants. A priority management issue for the Park should be to return the land to native vegetation. Efforts are already underway at some Park sites, such as the restoration of the ponderosa pine stand at Spalding and the reclamation of the borrow pit at White Bird Battlefield. These efforts are vital and should continue.

Other key management issues throughout the Park include increased encroachment and commercialization of surrounding areas, sustainability of water quality, federally listed threatened and endangered species, and wetland restoration or rehabilitation. The following comments are intended to address management issues on a site-by-site basis.

Buffalo Eddy

Management issues here include assessing the effects of recent road construction, which increases the potential mortality of birds from collisions with cars. In addition, access to the site is increasing on the Idaho side by boat. Residential and secondary homes are also encroaching on the Washington side. With the exception of exotics, the most likely impacts to birds here will come from human disturbance. Importantly, the deep draws between the ridges at this site are dominated by hackberry and provide important nesting habitat and cover for breeding birds, and cover and forage for migrating and wintering birds. The power poles currently provide nest platforms for western kingbirds, but other structures could be erected for this species. The rock faces and cliffs provide habitat for nesting rock and canyon wrens, American kestrels, and swallow species.

Spalding

As mentioned above, exotic species and noxious weeds are the key issue here as well as encroachment from outside the Park boundary. I recommend that the Park continue its restoration efforts of the ponderosa pine stand as well as to work toward restoring the majority of the Park to native vegetation. Perhaps paradoxically, the arboretum, although comprised of many introduced species, provides valuable habitat to migrating and overwintering birds. Maintaining the water quality in Lapwai Creek should be a priority for species such as the spotted sandpiper and belted kingfisher. The viaduct provides a substrate for cliff swallows to build their nests. This should be protected from disturbance.

Heart of the Monster

Management issues here include exotic species and noxious weeds, and increased urbanization. Traffic on the highway poses risks to birds flying between the river and the wetland. The expansion of the RV park, which is one of the largest private campgrounds in Idaho, together with the construction of a motel and residential housing in recent years, has reduced the buffer near the eastern part of the site. Much of the site is harvested as grass hay during the summer, which eliminates habitat for birds and has the potential to disrupt breeding and/or cause mortality of young. If the public could be informed of the importance of this habitat to birds, then the existing walkway could be left, but the rest of the site could be restored to native vegetation. The riparian corridor, associated slough, and wetland result in a diverse assemblage of birds and should be maintained. The black locust stand opposite the highway and adjacent the wetland is species poor and could potentially be replaced with native species such as ponderosa pine and/or black cottonwood.

Lolo Trail and Lolo Pass/Musselshell Meadow

The most current and significant management issue for this site is the potential impact from increased traffic along this corridor, especially in relation to the Lewis and Clark bicentennial. Firewood gathering, the potential for introducing exotic species, and general disturbance to these sites are the most pressing management concerns. Other ongoing issues include timber extraction and the potential for inappropriate development at Musselshell Meadow. The Lolo Trail was the only site where I detected American three-toed woodpeckers. These woodpeckers nest and forage on dead and dying substrates. Firewood gathering should be either restricted or closely monitored, so as to limit impacts to this species as well as other cavity-nesting species such as the northern pygmy-owl. Camping should be limited to specific sites so as to reduce the impacts to surrounding areas.

White Bird Battlefield

This site has been severely impacted by exotic species and noxious weeds. It has lost many of the native grasses to yellow starthistle and as such has been rendered less suitable to species such as the grasshopper sparrow and savannah sparrow. The two species most observed in the yellow starthistle were the western meadowlark and gray partridge. But the majority of the other species were primarily restricted to the cliff areas, shrubby draws, riparian areas, and Swartz Pond. The riparian corridor along White Bird Creek would benefit from rehabilitation efforts and likely has water quality issues due to the significant commercial cattle operation on the opposite side of the creek. Swartz Pond provides important migratory and breeding habitat for birds, but because it draws so many birds, it also attracts the attention of gun enthusiasts who may illegally shoot birds. In 2002, a pair of tundra swans were shot and killed on the pond. This is primarily an issue of education. Perhaps placing some signs at the pond explaining the laws that protect migratory birds as well as the importance of these species would discourage such inappropriate activities.

Old Chief Joseph Gravesite

This is a small site that chiefly has a "manicured" appearance. Similar to Heart of the Monster, this site would benefit from restoration to native species. In addition, fishing on the lake adjacent the site poses threats to birds from discarded monofilament fishing line and plastic six-pack carriers. Signs should be placed near the lake edge to inform people of this risk and to request that they pick up any line and/or fishing tackle to prevent injuries or death to birds from ingestion or entanglement.

Bear Paw Battlefield

The unique ecological nature of Bear Paw Battlefield provides a refuge amidst a landscape of otherwise tilled and grazed land. Bear Paw is an island of native shortgrass prairie and as such provides important habitat to prairie dependent species such as the Baird's sparrow and Sprague's pipit. Both of these species have experienced population declines because of the conversion of their native prairie to cultivation, overgrazing, and invasion of exotic plants. Every effort should be made to assure that the integrity of this site be maintained without compromise. Visitors should be encouraged to stay on existing trails to limit habitat degradation and disturbance to ground-nesting birds. Exotic vegetation is an issue here and efforts should be made to maintain native vegetation. Habitat diversity should be maximized by managing for a range of grassland structure (height and density) and a variety of successional stages (Bachand 2001). Mowing and haying operations should be delayed to permit grassland bird nestlings to fledge.

Big Hole National Battlefield

Key management issues at Big Hole National Battlefield include adjacent agricultural and ranching land use, potential for cowbird parasitism, past fire suppression in the forested area, and the invasion of exotic species. Because of the diversity of habitats at this site, it supports a variety of bird communities, each with their inherent management issues. Management recommendations outlined for riparian (Idaho Partners in Flight 1998) and sagebrush (Paige and Ritter 1999) habitats should be incorporated into a management plan for the Park. Prescribed fire could be used as a tool to open up the canopy of the lodgepole dominated forest, but controlled burns should be restricted to the fall to avoid nesting season mortality. Visitors should be encouraged to stay on maintained trails to limit disturbance to nesting birds.

Conclusions

This inventory provides a foundation from which to build future avian research and monitoring efforts at Nez Perce National Historical Park. The logical next step is to integrate this information into a long-term monitoring plan that will be consistent with the goals established in the four major bird initiatives and tailored to the specific species and management issues at each site. Depending on the future objectives of the Park, more intensive efforts could be carried out to obtain demographic data at these sites. With all of the current efforts to integrate bird monitoring, this is an opportune time for the Park to collaborate with other agencies and organizations and to gradually develop a comprehensive understanding of the dynamics of bird communities within the Park.

Literature Cited

American Ornithologists' Union. 1998. Check-list of North American birds, 7th ed. American Ornithologists' Union, Washington, DC.

American Ornithologists' Union. 2000. Forty-second supplement to the American Ornithologists' Union, Check-list of North American birds. Auk **117**:847–858.

Banks, R. C., C. Cicero, J. L. Dunn, A. W. Kratter, P. C. Rasmussen, J. V. Remsen, Jr., J. D. Rising, and D. F. Stotz. 2002. Forty-third supplement to the American Ornithologists' Union, Check-list of North American birds. Auk **119**:897–906.

Banks, R. C., C. Cicero, J. L. Dunn, A. W. Kratter, P. C. Rasmussen, J. V. Remsen, Jr., J. D. Rising, and D. F. Stotz. 2003. Forty-fourth supplement to the American Ornithologists' Union, Check-list of North American birds. Auk **120**:923–931.

Banks, R. C., C. Cicero, J. L. Dunn, A. W. Kratter, P. C. Rasmussen, J. V. Remsen, Jr., J. D. Rising, and D. F. Stotz. 2004. Forty-fifth supplement to the American Ornithologists' Union, Check-list of North American birds. Auk **121**:985–995.

Bachand, R. R. 2001. The American prairie: Going, going, gone? A status report on the American prairie. National Wildlife Federation, Rocky Mountain Natural Resource Center, Boulder, CO.

Bailey, R. G. 1995. Description of the ecoregions of the United States, 2nd ed., revised and expanded from 1st ed. of 1980. Misc. publication 1391 (rev.) with separate map at 1:7,500,000. WA.

Bechard, M. J. and J. K. Schmutz. 1995. Ferruginous hawk (*Buteo regalis*). Pages 1-19 *in* The birds of North America, No. 172 (A. Poole and F. Gill, eds.). The Academy of Natural Sciences, Philadelphia and The American Ornithologists' Union, Washington, D.C.

Bock, C. E., and J. E. Bock. 1987. Avian habitat occupancy following fire in a Montana shrubsteppe. Prairie Naturalist **19**:153-158.

Bock, C. E., and B. Webb. 1984. Birds as grazing indicator species in southeastern Arizona. J. Wildl. Manage. **48**:1045-1049.

Braun, C. E., M. F. Baker, R. L. Eng., J. S. Gashwiler, and M. H. Schroeder. 1976. Conservation committee report on effects of alteration of sagebrush communities on the associated avifauna. Wilson Bull **88**:165-171.

Buehler, D. A. 2000. Bald eagle (*Haliaeetus leucocephalus*). Pages 1-39 *in* The birds of North America, No. 506 (A. Poole and F. Gill, Eds.). The Birds of North America, Inc., Philadelphia, PA.

Burger, J. 1972. Dispersal and post-fledging survival of Franklin's gulls. Bird Banding **43**:267-275.

Burger, J., and M. Gochfeld. 1994. Franklin's gull (*Larus pipixcan*). *In* the Birds of North America, No. 116 (A. Poole and F. Gill, Eds.). Philadelphia: The Academy of Natural Sciences; Washington, D.C.: The American Ornithologists' Union.

Comer, P., D. Faber-Langendoen, R. Evans, S. Gawler, C. Josse, G. Kittel, S. Menard, M. Pyne, M. Reid, K. Schulz, K. Snow, and J. Teague. 2003. Ecological systems of the United States: a working classification of U.S. terrestrial systems. NatureServe, Arlington, VA.

Dale, B. 1990. The effect of haying on grassland passerines at Last Mtn. Lake Nat. Wildl. Area—1989. Unpublished report, Can. Wildl. Serv., Saskatoon, SK.

Dale, B. 1992. North American waterfowl management plan: implementation program related to non-game studies within the prairie habitat joint venture area. Annual report 1990-1991. Unpublished report, Can. Wildl. Serv., Saskatoon, SK.

Dale, B. 1993. 1992 Saskatchewan non-game evaluation of North American Waterfowl Management Plan. DNC and short grass cover—1992. Unpublished report, Sask. Wetland Conserv. Corp., Regina, SK.

Dale, B. C., P. A. Martin, and P. S. Taylor. 1997. Effects of hay management on grassland songbirds in Saskatchewan. Wildlife Society Bulletin. **25**:616-626.

Davis, S. K., D. C. Duncan, and M. A. Skeel. 1996. The Baird's sparrow: status resolved. Blue Jay **54**:185-191.

DeSante, D. F., K. M. Burton, P. Velez, and D. Froehlich. 2002. Maps manual 2002 protocol: Instructions for the establishment and operation of constant-effort bird-banding stations as part of the Monitoring Avian Productivity and Survivorship (MAPS) Program. Contribution number 127 of The Institute for Bird Populations, Point Reyes Station, CA.

Despain, D. G. 1973. Investigations into the vegetation of Big Hole Battlefield. Page 5 *in* Unpublished memorandum submitted to Big Hole National Battlefield.

DuMont, P. A. 1940. Relation of Franklin's gull colonies to agriculture on the Great Plains. Trans. North American Wildlife Conference **5**:183-189.

England, A. S., M. J. Bechard, and C. S. Houston. 1997. Swainson's hawk (*Buteo swainsoni*). Pages 1-27 *in* The birds of North America, No. 265 (A. Poole and F. Gill, eds.). The Academy of Natural Sciences, Philadelphia, PA and The American Ornithologists' Union, Washington, D.C.

Evans, R. M., and F. L. Knopf. 1993. American white pelican (*Pelecanus erythrorhynchos*). Pages 1-23 *in* The birds of North America, No. 57 (A. Poole and F. Gill, Eds.). The Academy of Natural Sciences, Philadelphia, PA and The American Ornithologists' Union, Washington, D.C.

Fitzner, R. E. 1980. Behavioral ecology of the Swainson's hawk (*Buteo swainsoni*). Washington Pacific NW Lab. PLN-2754.

Goossen, J. P., S. Brechtel, K. D. De Smet, D. Hjertass, and C. Werschler. 1993. Canadian Baird's sparrow recovery plan. Recovery of nationally endangered wildlife, report No. 3, Canadian Wildlife Federation, Ottawa, ON.

Green, M. T., P. E. Lowther, S. L. Jones, S. K. Davis, and B. C. Dale. 2002. Baird's sparrow (*Ammodramus bairdii*). Pages 1-19 *in* The birds of North America, No. 638 (A. Poole and F. Gill, eds.). The birds of North America, Inc., Philadelphia, PA.

Guay, J. W. 1968. The breeding biology of Franklin's gull (*Larus pipixcan*). Dissertation. University of Alberta, Edmonton, AB.

Harlow, D. L., and P. H. Bloom. 1989. Buteos and the golden eagle. Western raptor management symposium and workshop. National Wildlife Federation Science Technical Series **12**:102-110.

Hartley, M. J. 1994. Passerine abundance and productivity indices in grasslands managed for waterfowl nesting cover in Saskatchewan, Canada. Thesis. Louisiana State University, Baton Rouge, LA.

Herron, G. B., C. A. Mortimore, and M. S. Rawlings. 1985. Nevada raptors: their biology and management. Nevada Department of Wildlife Biology Bulletin No. 8.

Hutto, R. L. 1995. Composition of bird communities following stand-replacement fires in northern Rocky Mountain (U.S.A.) conifer forests. Conservation Biology **9**:1041-1058.

Idaho Partners in Flight. 1998. Riparian riches: habitat management for birds in Idaho. Idaho.

Kantrud, H. A., and R. L. Kologiski. 1982. Effects of soils and grazing on breeding birds of uncultivated upland grasslands of the northern Great Plains. U.S. Deprtment of the Interior, Fish and Wildlife Service Restoration Report 15, Washington, D.C.

Knick, S. T., and J. T. Rotenberry. 1995. Landscape characteristics of shrubsteppe habitats and breeding passerine birds. Conservation Biology **9**:1059-1071.

Knopf, F. L. 1994. Avian assemblages on altered grasslands. Studies in Avian Biology **15**:247-257.

Lane, J. 1968. *Ammodramus bairdii* (Audubon). Baird's sparrow. Pages 745-765 *in* Life histories of North American cardinals, grosbeaks, buntings, towhees, finches, sparrows, and their allies (O.L. Austin, Jr., ed.). U.S. National Museum Bulletin 237 Pt. 2.

Leonard, D. L., Jr. 2001. Three-toed woodpecker (*Picoides tridactylus*). Pages 1-23 *in* The birds of North America, No. 588 (A. Poole and F. Gill, eds.). The Birds of North America, Inc., Philadelphia, PA.

Littlefield, C. D., and S. P. Thompson. 1981. History and status of the Franklin's gull on Malheur National Wildlife Refuge, Oregon. Great Basin Naturalist **41**:440-444.

Madden, E. M. 1996. Passerine communities and bird-habitat relationships on prescribe-burned, mixed-grass prairie in North Dakota. Thesis. Montana State University, Bozeman, MT.

Medin, D. E., B. L. Welch, and W. P. Clary. 2000. Bird habitat relationships along a Great Basin elevational gradient. U.S. Forest Service, Rocky Mountatin Research Station RMRS-RP-23.

Monello, R. J., and R. G. Wright. 1998. I. Exotic pest plant inventory, mapping, and priorities for control in parks in the Pacific northwest, and II. Initial bird and mammal survey results for parks in the Pacific northwest. USGS Idaho Cooperative Fish and Wildlife Research Unit, University of Idaho, Moscow, ID.

Montana Natural Heritage Program. 2004. Montana animal species of concern. MTNHP & MFWP. Helena, MT.

Mueggler, W. F., and W. L. Stewart. 1980. Grassland and shrubland habitat types of western Montana. U.S.D.A. Forest Service General Technical Report Int-66, Intermountain Forest and Range Experiment Station.

Mueller-Dombois, D. and H. Ellenberg. 1974. Aims and methods of vegetation ecology. John Wiley and Sons, Inc., New York.

NatureServe. 2003. Ecological Systems Database, version 1.02. NatureServe, Arlington, VA.

Olendorff, R. R. 1993. Status, biology, and management of ferruginous hawks: a review. Raptor Research and Technical Assistance Center Species Report, U.S. Department of the Interior, Bureau of Land Management, Boise, ID.

Owens, R. A., and M. T. Myres. 1973. Effects of agriculture upon populations of native passerine birds of an Alberta fescue grassland. Canadian Journal of Zoology 51:697-713.

Paige, C., and S. A. Ritter. 1999. Birds in a sagebrush sea: Managing sagebrush habitats for bird communities. Partners in Flight Western Working Group, Boise, ID.

Patil, S. A., J. L. Kovner, and K. P. Burnham. 1982. Optimum nonparametric estimation of population density based on ordered distances. Biometrics 38:243-248.

Payette National Forest. 1993. Region 4 sensitive species broadcast vocalization compact disc. CD use information, (S. Jeffries and L. Ostermiler, technical coordinators.). Payette National Forest, McCall, ID.

Pierce, J. R. 1982. A floristic study of the Big Hole National Battlefield. Thesis. University of Montana, Missoula, MT.

Prescott, D. R. C., and G. M. Wagner. 1996. Avian responses to implementation of a complimentary/rotational grazing system by the North American Waterfowl Management Plan in southern Alberta: the Medicine Wheel project. Alberta NAWMP Centre. NAWMP-018. Edmonton, AB.

Ralph, C. J., G. R. Geupel, P. Pyle, T. E. Martin, and D. F. DeSante. 1993. Handbook of field methods for monitoring landbirds. Page 21 *in* General Technical Report PSW-GTR-144. Albany, CA: Pacific Southwest Research Station, Forest Service, U.S. Department of Agriculture.

Ralph, C. J., S. Droege, and J. R. Sauer. 1995. Managing and monitoring birds using point counts: standards and applications. Pages 161-175 *in* Monitoring bird populations by point counts (C. J. Ralph, J. R. Sauer, and S. Droege, technical eds). General Technical Report PSW-GTR-149. Albany, CA: Pacific Southwest Research Station, Forest Service, U.S. Department of Agriculture.

Ratti, J. T., and E. O. Garton. 1996. Research and Experimental Design. Pages 1-23 *in* Research and management techniques for wildlife and habitats (T. A. Bookhout, ed.). 5th ed., revised. The Wildlife Society, Bethesda, MD.

Robbins, M. B., and B. C. Dale. 1999. Sprague's pipit (*Anthus spragueii*). Pages 1-15 *in* the birds of North America, No. 439 (A. Poole and F. Gill, eds.). The Birds of North America, Inc., Philadelphia, PA.

Rotenberry, J. T. 1998. Avian conservation research needs in western shrublands: exotic invaders and the alteration of ecosystem processes. Pages 261-272 *in* Avian conservation: research and management (J. M. Marzluff and R. Sallabanks, eds.). Island Press, Covelo, CA.

Rotenberry, J. T., M. A. Patten, and K. L. Preston. 1999. Brewer's sparrow (*Spizella breweri*). Pages 1-23 *in* The birds of North America, No. 390 (A. Poole and F. Gill, eds.). The Birds of North America, Inc., Philadelphia, PA.

Samson, F., and F. Knopf. 1994. Prairie conservation in North America. BioScience **44**:418-421.

Shriver, W. G., P. D. Vickery, and S. A. Hedges. 1996. Effects of summer burns on Florida grasshopper sparrows. Florida Field Naturalist; in press.

Stedman, S. J. 2000. Horned grebe (*Podiceps auritus*). Pages 1-27 *in* The birds of North America, No. 505 (A. Poole and F. Gill, eds.). The Birds of North America, Inc., Philadelphia, PA.

Stephens, D. A., and S. H. Sturts. 1998. Idaho bird distribution. Special Publicaton No. 13. 2nd edition. Idaho Museum of Natural History and Idaho Department of Fish and Game.

Stewart, R. E. 1975. Breeding birds of North Dakota. Tri-College Center, Environmental Studies, Fargo, ND.

Suter, G. W., II., and J. L. Jones. 1980. Criteria for golden eagle, ferruginous hawk, and prairie falcon nest site protection. Raptor Restoration **15**:12-18.

U.S. Department of the Interior, National Park Service. 1997. General management plan: Nez Perce National Historical Park and Big Hole National Battlefield. Prepared by J. W. Powell, P. Henderson, M. Marek, S. Durrant, D. Kodak, C. Hawkes, B. Clemensen, L. Domler, and H. Thompson. Nez Perce National Historical Park, Spalding, ID.

Van Sickle, W. 1987. Survey of Vertebrates on the Big Hole National Battlefield. Report 88-01, Wyoming Cooperative Fishery and Wildlife Research Unit, Laramie, WY.

Vickery, P. D. 1996. Grasshopper sparrow (*Ammodramus savannarum*). Pages 1-23 *in* The birds of North America, No. 239 (A. Poole and F. Gill, Eds.). The Academy of Natural Sciences, Philadelphia, PA and The American Ornithologists' Union, Washington, D.C.

Vickery, P. D., J. R. Herkert, F. L. Knopf, J. Ruth, and C. E. Keller. In press. Grassland birds: an overview of threats and recommended management strategies. Partners-in-Flight Conference, Cape May, NJ.

White, C. M., and T. L. Thurow. 1985. Reproduction of ferruginous hawks exposed to controlled disturbance. Condor **87**:14-22.

Wilson, S. D., and J. W. Belcher. 1989. Plant and bird communities of native prairie and introduced Eurasian vegetation in Manitoba, Canada. Conservation Biology **3**:39-44.

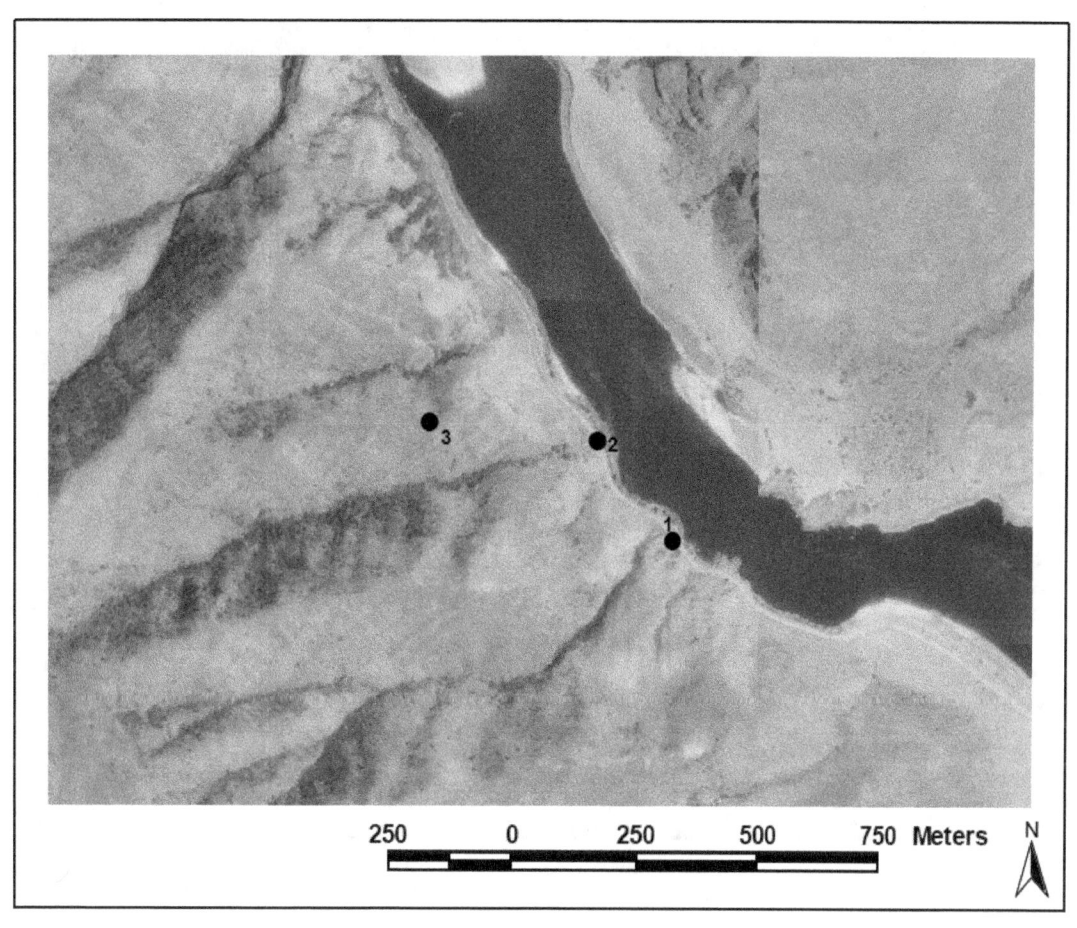

Figure 1. Location of point count stations at Buffalo Eddy, USGS Quads: Captain John Rapids, Idaho-Washington.

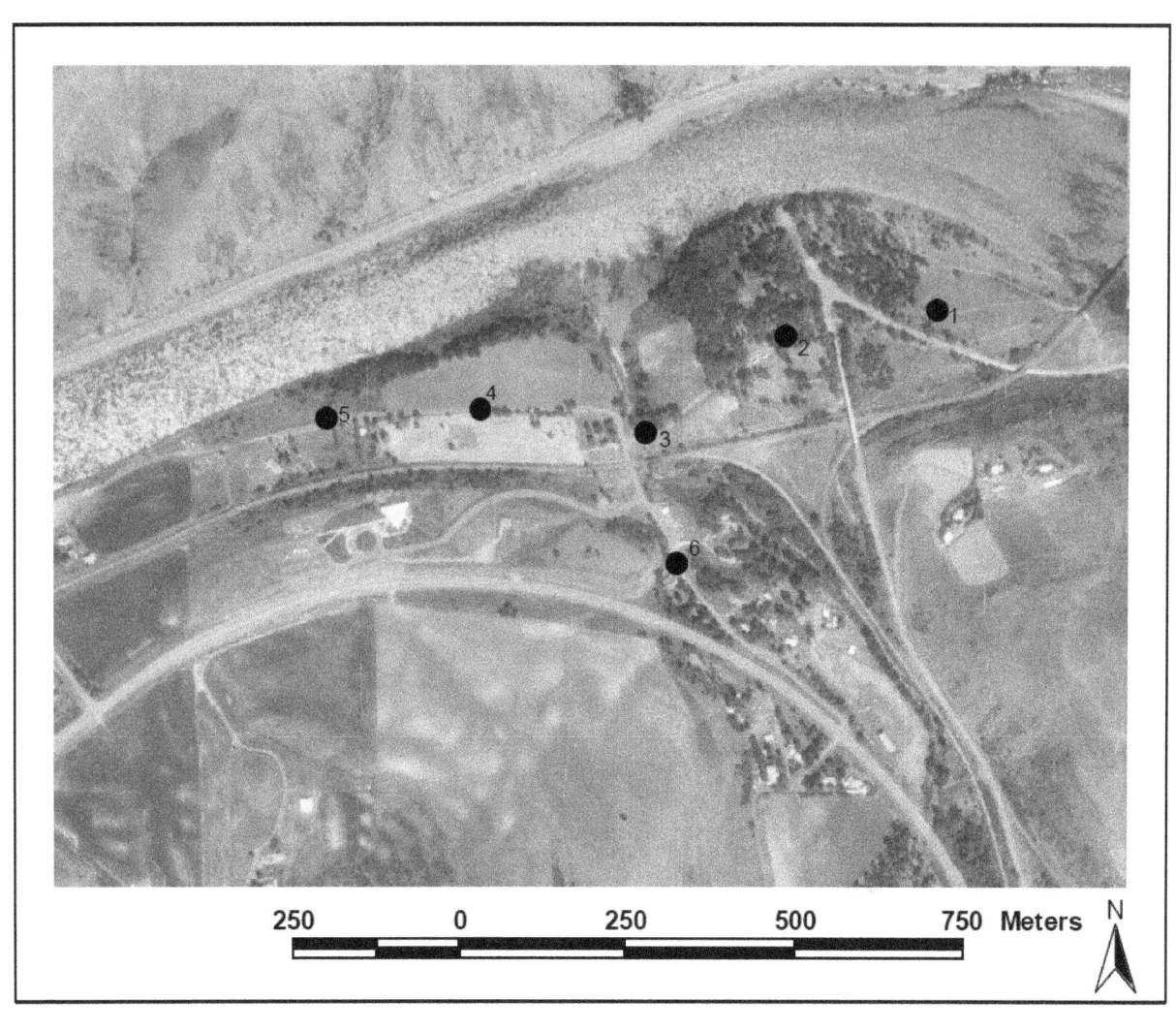

Figure 2. Location of point count stations at Spalding, USGS Quad: Lapwai, Idaho.

36

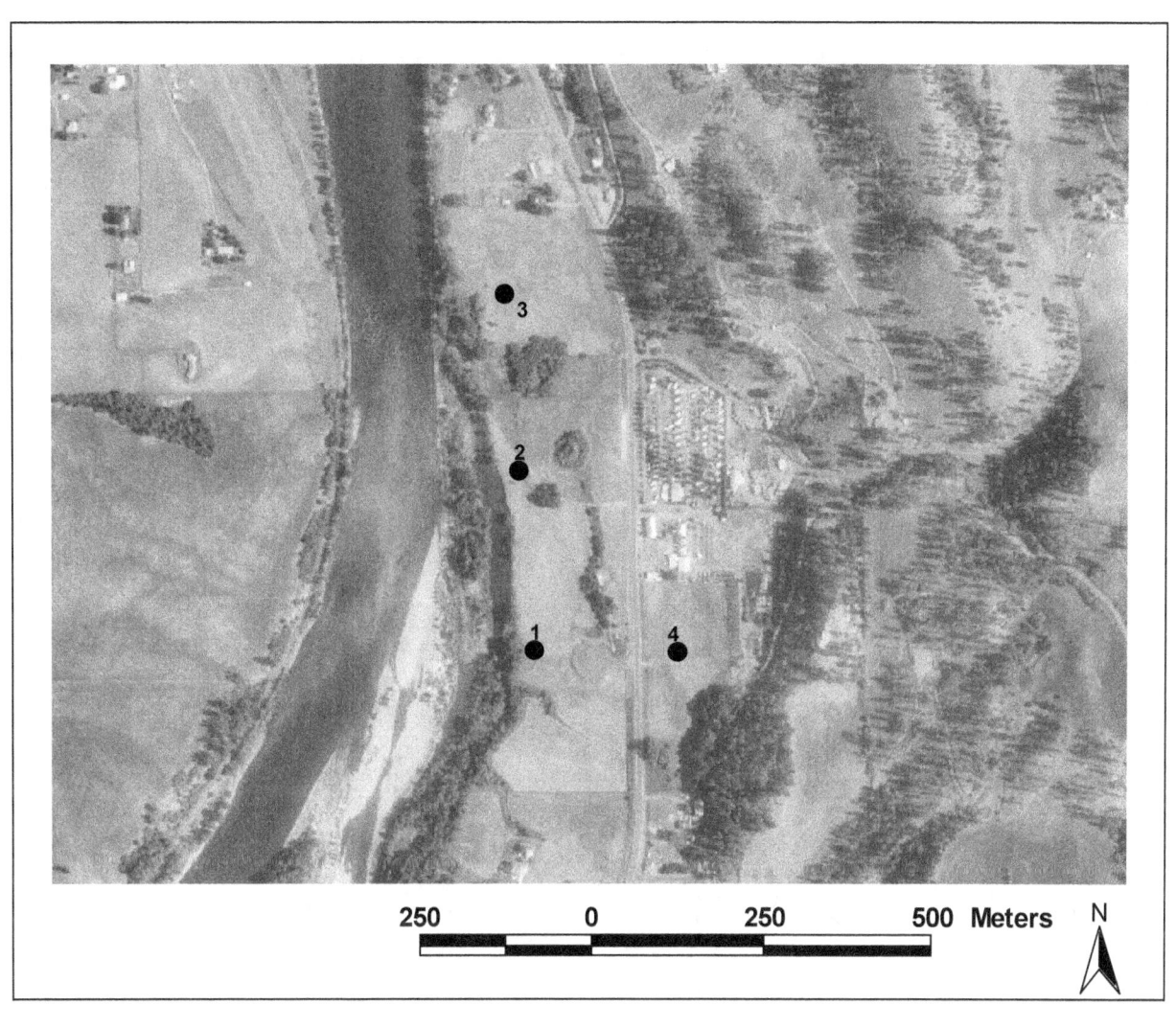

Figure 3. Location of point count stations at Heart of the Monster, USGS Quads: Kamiah, Kooskia, Idaho.

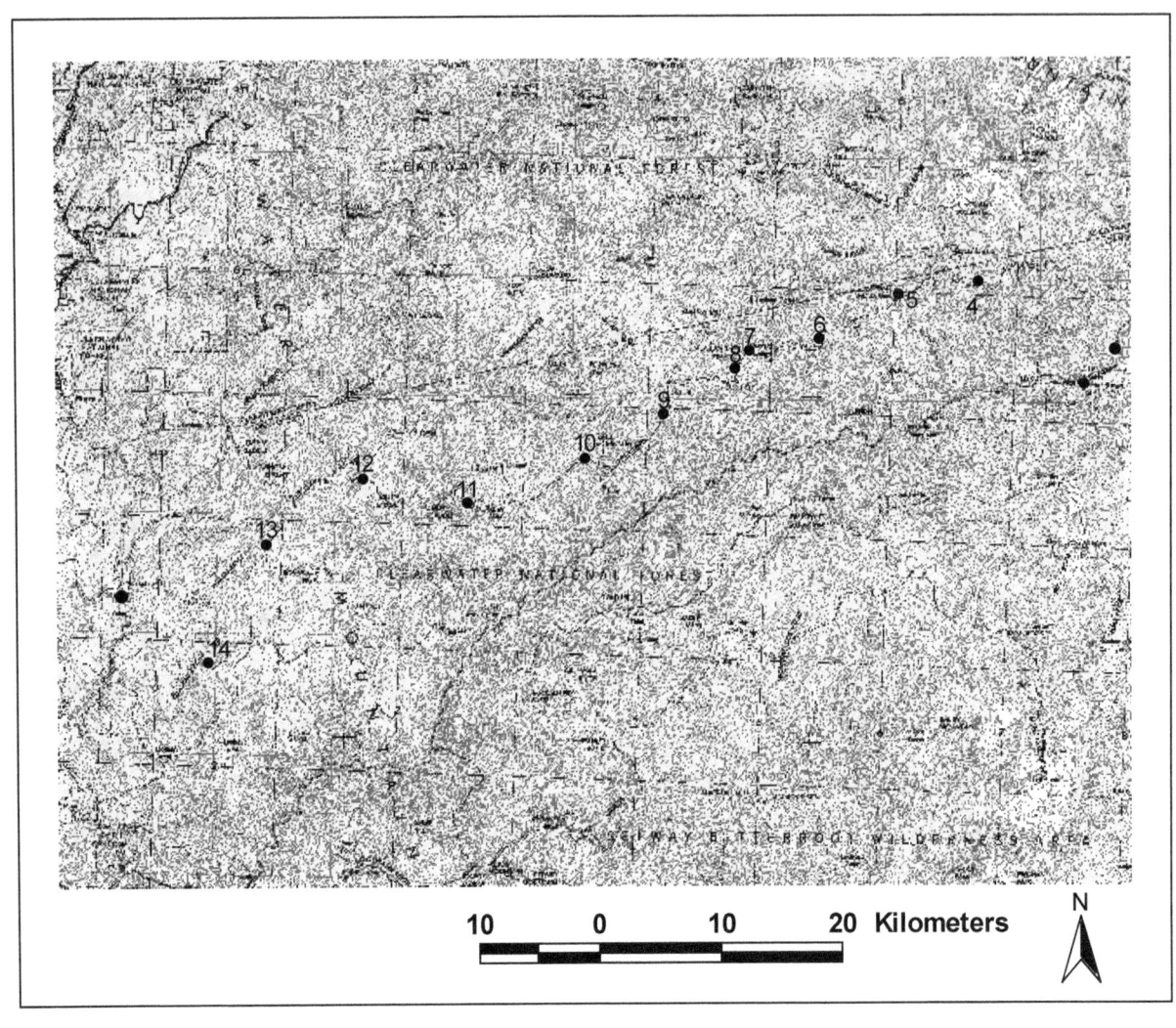

Figure 4. Location of point count stations at Lolo Trail and Lolo Pass/Musselshell Meadow, USGS 1:250,000: Hamilton, Montana and Idaho.

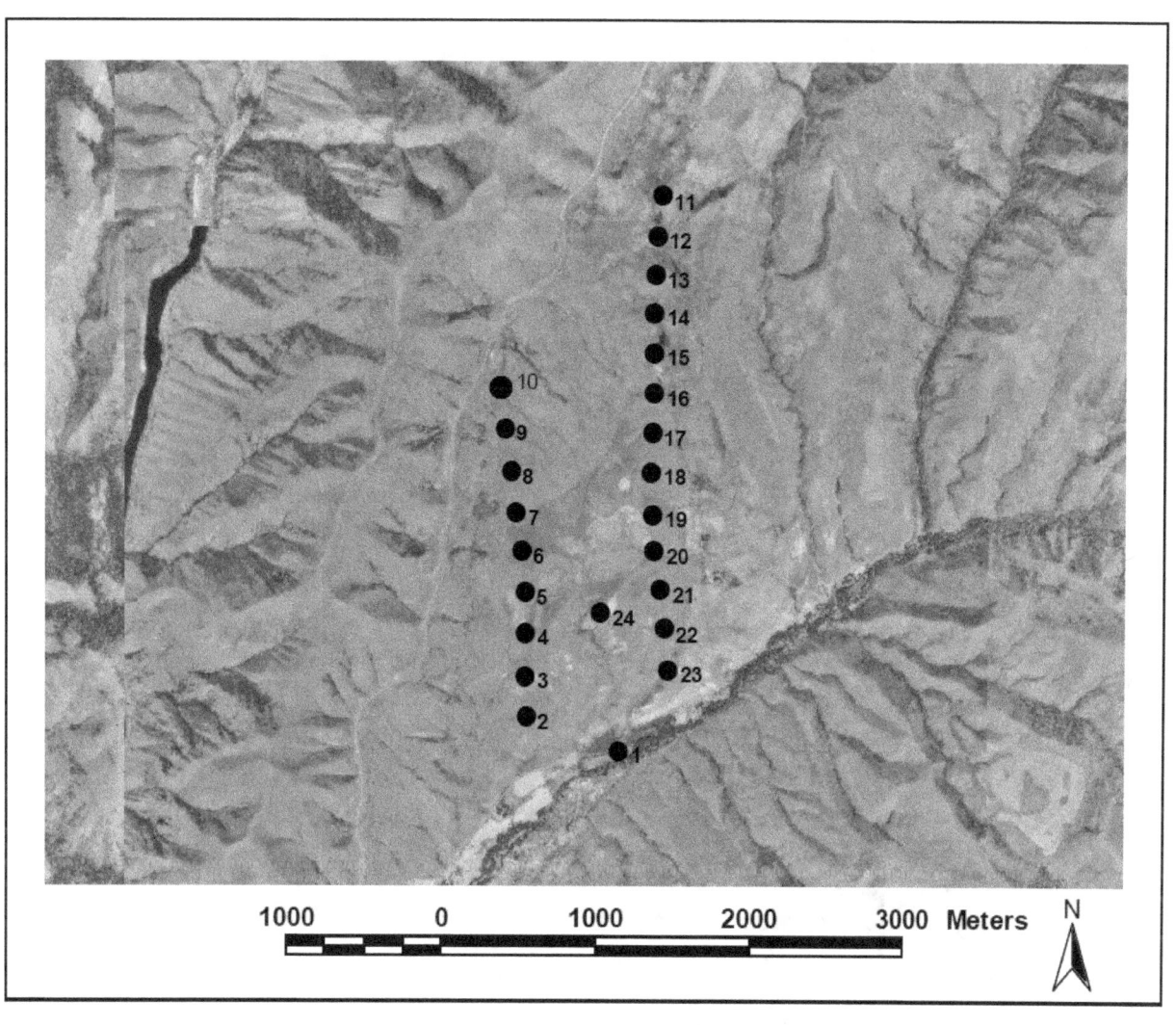

Figure 5. Location of point count stations at White Bird Battlefield, USGS Quads: White Bird, White Bird Hill, Idaho.

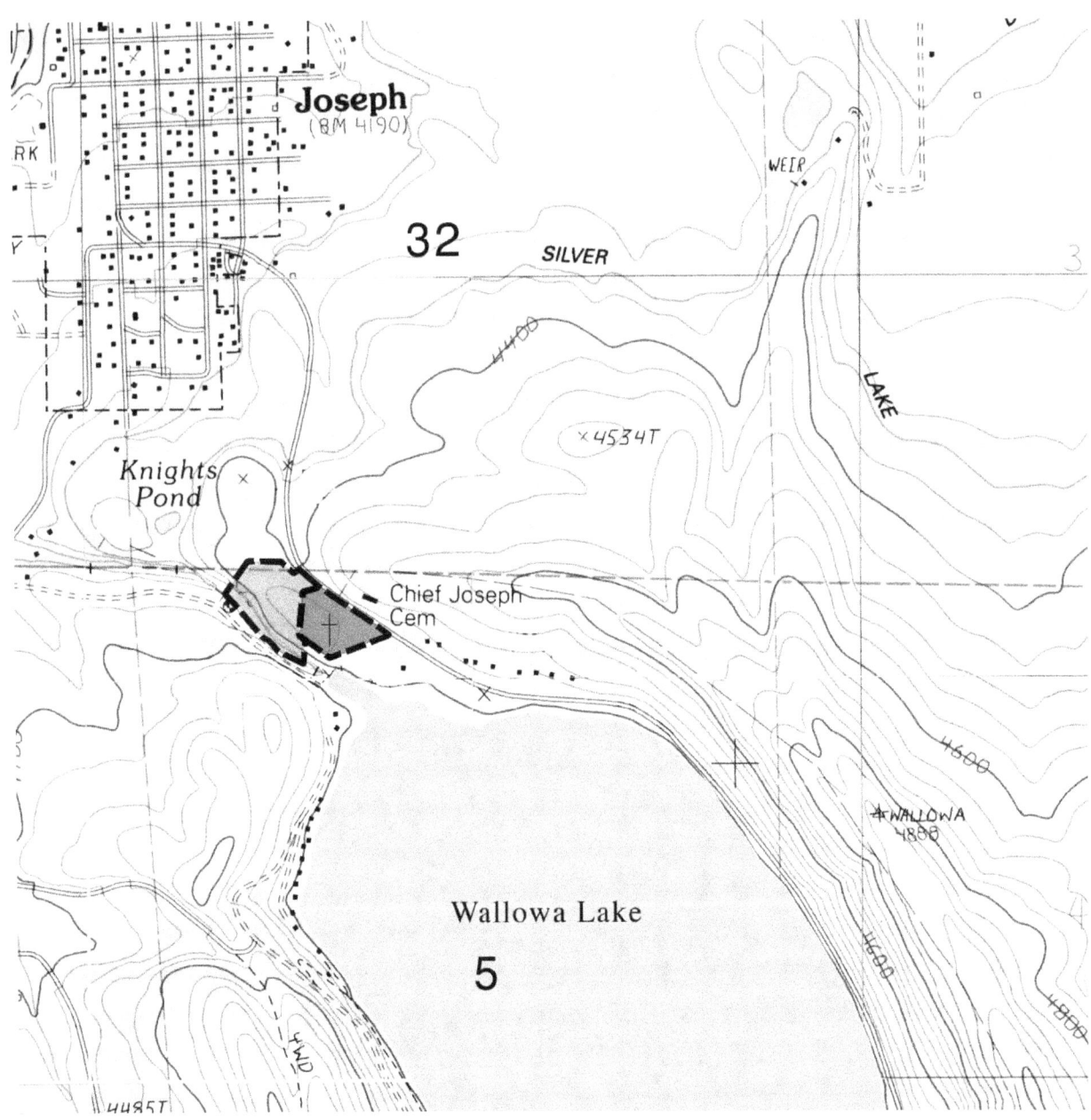

Figure 6. Location of point count station at Old Chief Joseph Gravesite, USGS Quad: Joseph, Oregon.

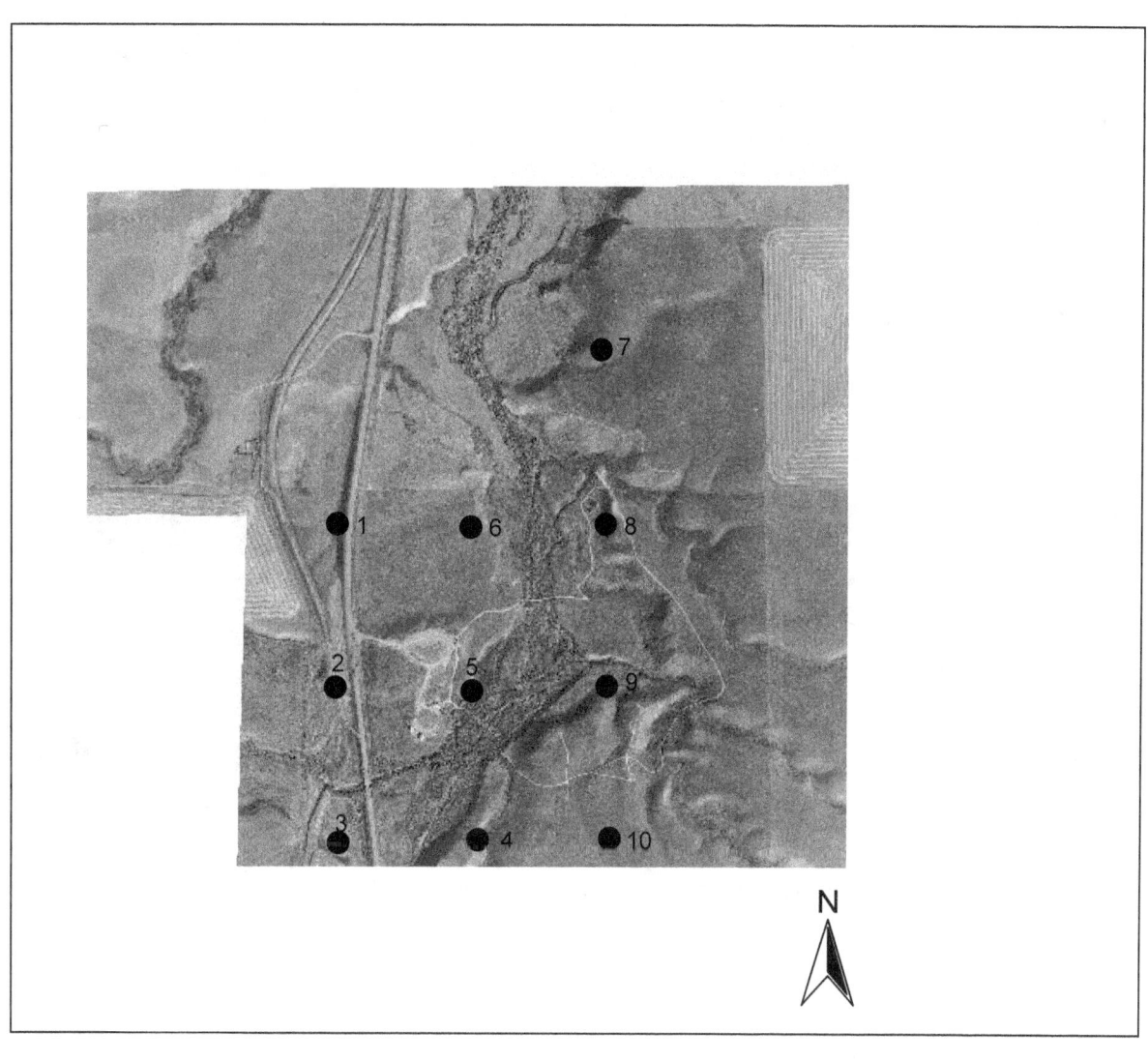

Figure 7. Location of point count stations at Bear Paw Battlefield, USGS Quads: Cleveland NW, Cleveland, Montana.

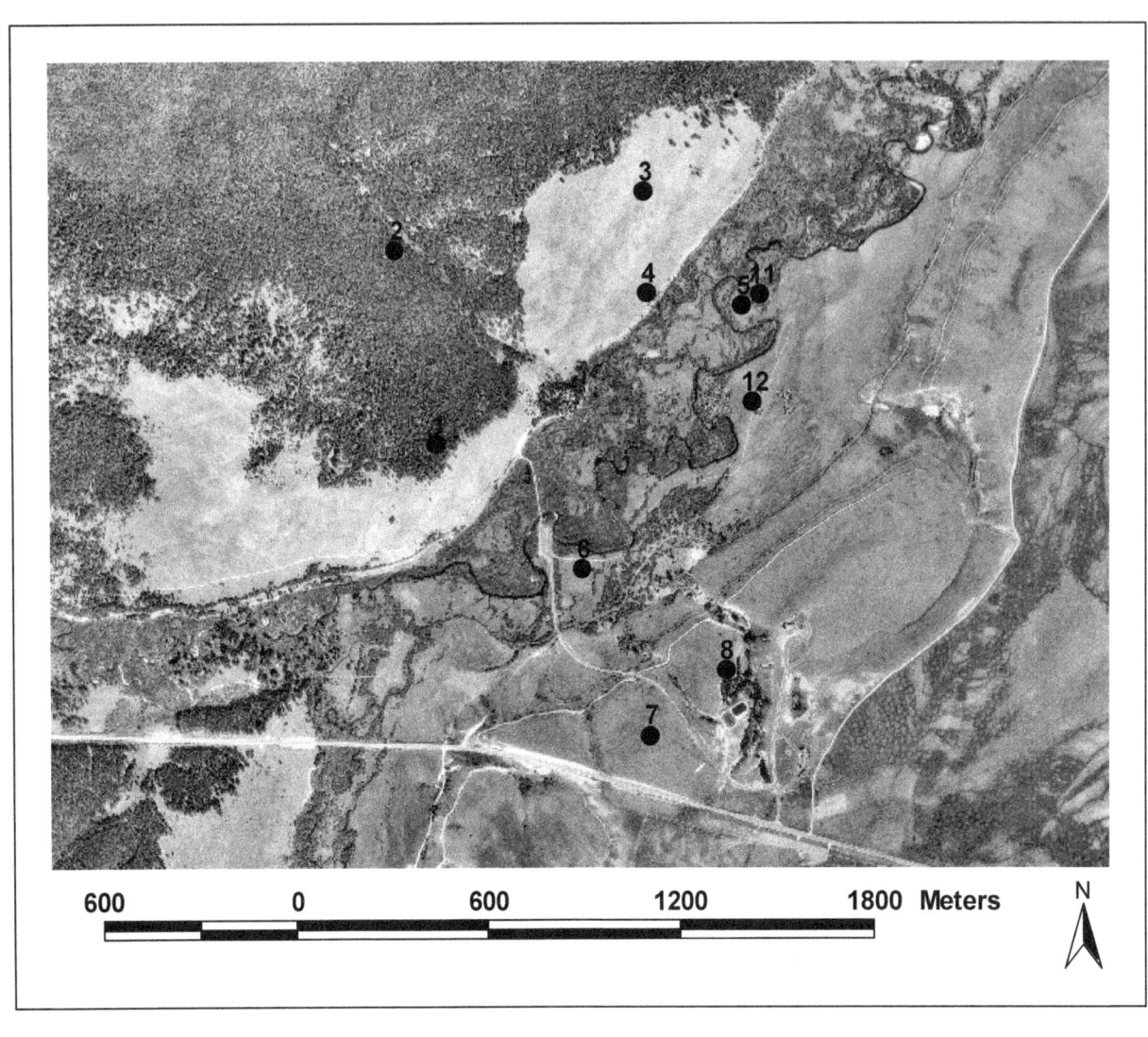

Figure 8. Location of point count stations at Big Hole National Battlefield, USGS Quad: Big Hole Battlefield, Montana.

Figure 9. Whitman Mission National Historic Site, USGS Quad: College Place, Washington.

Table 1. Relative abundances of 43 bird species at Buffalo Eddy, Asotin County, Washington, from January 26, 1999 to December 19, 1999; 4 = abundant, 3 = common, 2 = uncommon or infrequent, 1 = rare; also shown are mean point count results and breeding status.

Species	Total #[a]	Birds/Count Period[a]	Density (Birds/ha)[a]	90% CI[a]	Total #[b]	% of Total[b]	Abundance Category	Breeding Status[c]
Canada goose					13	7.3	4	T
Common merganser					1	0.6	2	M
Northern harrier					5	2.8	3	B
Cooper's hawk[d]							2	T
Red-tailed hawk					3	1.7	3	T
Golden eagle					1	0.6	2	T
American kestrel					10	5.6	4	B
Chukar					8	4.5	3	L
Gray partridge					2	1.1	2	B
California quail	1	0.11			1	0.6	2	L
Killdeer[d]							2	M
Rock pigeon					9	5.1	4	L
Mourning dove					2	1.1	2	L
Western screech-owl[d]							2	M
Common nighthawkl[d]							2	T
Unidentified hummingbird[d]							1	M
Belted kingfisher	1	0.11			1	0.6	2	T
Northern flicker					2	1.1	2	T
Willow flycatcher[d]							1	T
Western kingbird	2	0.22	0.053	0.079	6	3.4	3	B
Black-billed magpie	1	0.11			2	1.1	2	T
American crow					18	10.2	4	L
Violet-green swallow					9	5.1	4	L
Black-capped chickadee					1	0.6	2	M
Rock wren	1	0.11			5	2.8	3	B
Canyon wren					19	10.7	4	B
Bewick's wren[d]							1	T
Winter wren[d]							1	M
Golden-crowned kinglet[d]							1	M
Ruby-crowned kinglet[d]							1	M
Yellow warbler	6	0.67	0.314	0.274	6	3.4	3	L
Yellow-rumped warbler[d]							1	M
MacGillivray's warbler					1	0.6	2	M
Yellow-breasted chat					2	1.1	2	L
Spotted towhee	2	0.22			9	5.1	4	L
Song sparrow	8	0.89	0.605	0.515	16	9.0	4	B
Dark-eyed junco[d]							1	M
Black-headed grosbeak	1	0.11			2	1.1	2	L
Lazuli bunting	5	0.56	0.307	0.313	9	5.1	4	B
Red-winged blackbird					2	1.1	2	M

Table 1. Relative abundances of 43 bird species at Buffalo Eddy, Asotin County, Washington, from 26 January 1999 to 19 December 1999 (continued).

Species	Total #[a]	Birds/Count Period[a]	Density (Birds/ha)[a]	90% CI[a]	Total #[b]	% of Total[b]	Abundance Category	Breeding Status[c]
Western meadowlark[d]							1	T
Brown-headed cowbird	1	0.11			5	2.8	3	T
American goldfinch	1	0.11			7	4.0	3	L

[a] Breeding season point count results (data truncated at 100 m). Sample sizes of one were too small for density analysis and were eliminated from the table.
[b] Total number recorded and percent of total based on unlimited distance point counts.
[c] B = Breeder; L = Likely Breeder; T = Transient; M = Migrant.
[d] Encountered outside of point counts.

Table 2. Relative abundances of 69 bird species at Spalding, Nez Perce County, Idaho, from January 28, 1999 to December 20, 1999; 4 = abundant, 3 = common, 2 = uncommon or infrequent, 1 = rare; also shown are mean point count results and breeding status.

Species	Total #[a]	Birds/Count Period[a]	Density (Birds/ha)[a]	90% CI[a]	Total #[b]	% of Total[b]	Abundance Category	Breeding Status[c]
Great blue heron					2	0.3	2	T
Canada goose					38	5.8	4	L
Wood duck[d]							1	T
Mallard					9	1.4	3	B
Common merganser	1	0.06			1	0.2	2	B
Northern harrier					1	0.2	2	T
Sharp-shinned hawk[d]							1	T
Cooper's hawk					1	0.2	2	T
Red-tailed hawk					4	0.6	3	L
American kestrel	8	0.44	0.250	0.207	16	2.5	4	B
Chukar					1	0.2	2	T
Ring-necked pheasant	1	0.06			3	0.5	2	T
Wild turkey					11	1.7	3	T
California quail	16	0.89	0.579	0.354	47	7.2	4	L
Killdeer	2	0.11	0.065	0.085	6	0.9	3	L
Spotted sandpiper	3	0.17	0.100	0.112	4	0.6	3	L
Wilson's snipe[d]							1	T
Ring-billed gull					7	1.1	3	T
California gull					8	1.2	3	T
Rock pigeon					27	4.1	4	T
Mourning dove	5	0.28	0.229	0.221	13	2.0	4	L
Barn owl[d]							1	L
Great horned owl					1	0.2	2	B
Common nighthawk					5	0.8	3	T
Belted kingfisher					6	0.9	3	T
Downy woodpecker					2	0.3	2	L
Northern flicker	3	0.17	0.100	0.112	12	1.8	3	L
Western wood-pewee	9	0.50	0.173	0.128	17	2.6	4	L
Willow flycatcher[d]							1	T
Cordilleran flycatcher	5	0.28	0.229	0.213	5	0.8	3	T
Western kingbird	7	0.39	0.540	0.538	7	1.1	3	B
Warbling vireo	2	0.11	0.146	0.190	2	0.3	2	L
Red-eyed vireo	2	0.11	0.016	0.021	3	0.5	2	L

Table 2. Relative abundances of 69 bird species at Spalding, Nez Perce County, Idaho, from January 28, 1999 to December 20, 1999 (continued).

Species	Total #[a]	Birds/ Count Period[a]	Density (Birds/ha)[a]	90% CI[a]	Total #[b]	% of Total[b]	Abundance Category	Breeding Status[c]
Black-billed magpie	1	0.06			19	2.9	4	L
American crow					7	1.1	3	T
Common raven	1	0.06			6	0.9	3	T
Violet-green swallow[d]							1	T
Northern rough-winged swallow					3	0.5	2	M
Cliff swallow					2	0.3	2	B
Black-capped chickadee	1	0.06			5	0.8	3	L
Brown creeper[d]							1	M
Bewick's wren	2	0.11	0.146	0.190	10	1.5	3	B
House wren	11	0.61	1.141	0.846	11	1.7	3	L
Golden-crowned kinglet[d]							1	M
Townsend's solitaire[d]							1	M
American robin	38	2.11	3.411	1.942	74	11.3	4	B
Gray catbird					1	0.2	2	L
European starling	24	1.33	2.301	1.784	96	14.7	4	L
Cedar waxwing	7	0.39	6.620	7.176	22	3.4	4	B
Yellow warbler	19	1.06	0.833	0.481	20	3.1	4	L
Yellow-rumped warbler[d]							1	M
MacGillivray's warbler	1	0.06			1	0.2	2	M
Yellow-breasted chat					1	0.2	2	T
Western tanager	5	0.28	0.742	0.716	5	0.8	3	L
Spotted towhee					1	0.2	2	T
Chipping sparrow					1	0.2	2	L
Song sparrow	9	0.50	0.236	0.175	22	3.4	4	B
White-crowned sparrow[d]							1	M
Dark-eyed junco					1	0.2	2	M
Black-headed grosbeak	3	0.17	1.107	1.244	3	0.5	2	L
Lazuli bunting[d]							1	T
Red-winged blackbird	5	0.28	0.186	0.185	32	4.9	4	L
Western meadowlark[d]							1	T
Brewer's blackbird	14	0.78	3.209	3.821	25	3.8	4	B
Brown-headed cowbird	4	0.22	0.399	0.419	4	0.6	3	L
Bullock's oriole	9	0.50	1.358	1.070	10	1.5	3	B
Cassin's finch[d]							1	M
House finch					1	0.2	2	L
American goldfinch	2	0.11	0.328	0.428	11	1.7	3	L

[a] Breeding season point count results (data truncated at 100 m). Sample sizes of one were too small for density analysis and were eliminated from the table.
[b] Total number recorded and percent of total based on unlimited distance point counts.
[c] B = Breeder; L = Likely Breeder; T = Transient; M = Migrant.
[d] Encountered outside of point counts.

48

Table 3. Relative abundances of 64 bird species at Heart of the Monster, Idaho County, Idaho, from January 29, 1999 to December 20, 1999; 4 = abundant, 3 = common, 2 = uncommon or infrequent, 1 = rare; also shown are mean point count results and breeding status.

Species	Total #[a]	Birds/Count Period[a]	Density (Birds/ha)[a]	90% CI[a]	Total #[b]	% of Total[b]	Abundance Category	Breeding Status[c]
Great blue heron					5	0.8	3	T
Canada goose	11	1.38	0.411	0.836	52	8.6	4	B
Wood duck[d]							2	T
Mallard	5	0.63	2.610	4.088	121	20.1	4	L
Northern shoveler[d]							2	M
Green-winged teal[d]							2	M
Ring-necked duck					2	0.3	2	M
Bufflehead					4	0.7	3	M
Common goldeneye					11	1.8	3	M
Hooded merganser[d]							2	M
Common merganser					1	0.2	2	L
Osprey					2	0.3	2	T
Cooper's hawk[d]							1	T
Red-tailed hawk					2	0.3	2	T
Ring-necked pheasant					7	1.2	3	L
California quail					28	4.7	4	L
American coot[d]							1	T
Killdeer	5	0.63	0.852	1.153	17	2.8	4	L
Spotted sandpiper	1	0.13			3	0.5	3	L
Wilson's snipe					7	1.2	3	T
Mourning dove					3	0.5	3	L
Western screech-owl[d]							1	T
Calliope hummingbird[d]							1	T
Belted kingfisher					9	1.5	3	L
Red-naped sapsucker[d]							1	M
Downy woodpecker					3	0.5	3	L
Northern flicker					14	2.3	4	L
Western wood-pewee	2	0.25			13	2.2	4	B
Willow flycatcher					4	0.7	3	T
Western kingbird							1	B
Eastern kingbird					2	0.3	2	T

Table 3. Relative abundances of 64 bird species at Heart of the Monster, Idaho County, Idaho, from January 29, 1999 to December 20, 1999 (continued).

Species	Total #[a]	Birds/Count Period[a]	Density (Birds/ha)[a]	90% CI[a]	Total #[b]	% of Total[b]	Abundance Category	Breeding Status[c]
Red-eyed vireo					3	0.5	3	T
Black-billed magpie					1	0.2	2	T
American crow[d]							1	T
Common raven					2	0.3	2	T
Tree swallow	1	0.13			3	0.5	3	B
Violet-green swallow					13	2.2	4	L
Northern rough-winged swallow	1	0.13			6	1.0	3	L
Black-capped chickadee					2	0.3	2	M
Bewick's wren					5	0.8	3	T
House wren[d]							1	T
Winter wren[d]							1	M
Western bluebird[d]							1	L
Mountain bluebird					3	0.5	3	M
American robin	5	0.63	0.852	0.807	39	6.5	4	B
Gray catbird	1	0.13			7	1.2	3	L
European starling					10	1.7	3	L
Cedar waxwing	1	0.13			62	10.3	4	B
Yellow warbler	16	2.00	0.771	0.513	30	5.0	4	L
Yellow-rumped warbler					1	0.2	2	M
MacGillivray's warbler[d]							1	M
Spotted towhee					1	0.2	2	T
Song sparrow	7	0.88	0.304	0.260	22	3.7	4	B
White-crowned sparrow[d]							1	M
Dark-eyed junco[d]							1	M
Black-headed grosbeak	2	0.25	0.041	0.056	4	0.7	3	L
Red-winged blackbird	13	1.63	0.639	0.601	32	5.3	4	L
Brewer's blackbird	2	0.25	1.311	1.963	13	2.2	3	B
Brown-headed cowbird	11	1.38	2.568	2.782	15	2.5	4	B
Bullock's oriole	1	0.13			1	0.2	2	M
House finch					4	0.7	3	L
Red crossbill					1	0.2	2	M
Pine siskin					1	0.2	2	M
American goldfinch	1	0.13			11	1.8	3	L

[a] Breeding season point count results (data truncated at 100 m). Sample sizes of one were too small for density analysis and were eliminated from the table.
[b] Total number recorded and percent of total based on unlimited distance point counts.
[c] B = Breeder; L = Likely Breeder; T = Transient; M = Migrant.
[d] Encountered outside of point counts.

Table 4. Relative abundances of 66 bird species along the Lolo Trail and Lolo Pass/Musselshell Meadow, Clearwater and Idaho Counties, Idaho, from July 28, 1999 to October 5, 1999; 4 = abundant, 3 = common, 2 = uncommon or infrequent, 1 = rare; also shown is breeding status.

Species	Total Recorded[a]	% of Total[a]	Abundance Category	Breeding Status[b]
Turkey vulture[c]			2	T
Mallard	1	0.9	2	T
Green-winged teal[c]			2	T
Bufflehead[c]			2	T
Osprey[c]			2	T
Red-tailed hawk	2	1.8	3	T
American kestrel[c]			2	T
Spruce grouse[c]			2	B
Mourning dove[c]			2	T
Great horned owl[c]			2	T
Northern pygmy-owl[c]			2	T
Common nighthawk[c]			2	T
Vaux's swift[c]			2	T
Rufous hummingbird[c]			2	L
Belted kingfisher[c]			2	T
Red-naped sapsucker[c]			2	T
Hairy woodpecker[c]			2	L
American three-toed woodpecker	1	0.9	2	B
Northern flicker	4	3.5	4	L
Pileated woodpecker[c]			2	T
Olive-sided flycatcher	2	1.8	3	L
Western wood-pewee[c]			2	T
Willow flycatcher	1	0.9	2	L
Hammond's flycatcher[c]			2	T
Dusky flycatcher[c]			2	T
Warbling vireo	2	1.8	3	L
Gray jay[c]			2	L
Steller's jay[c]			2	L
Clark's nutcracker[c]			1	T
Common raven	1	0.9	2	L
Violet-green swallow[c]			1	T
Northern rough-winged swallow[c]			1	B
Barn swallow	2	1.8	3	T

Table 4. Relative abundances of 66 bird species along the Lolo Trail and Lolo Pass/Musselshell Meadow, Clearwater and Idaho Counties, Idaho, from July 28, 1999 to October 5, 1999 (continued).

Species	Total #[a]	% of Total[a]	Abundance Category	Breeding Status[b]
Mountain chickadee	5	4.4	4	L
Chestnut-backed chickadee	1	0.9	2	L
Red-breasted nuthatch	3	2.6	3	L
Brown creeper	2	1.8	3	T
House wren	1	0.9	2	L
Winter wren	4	3.5	4	B
American dipper[c]			1	T
Golden-crowned kinglet	7	6.1	4	L
Ruby-crowned kinglet[c]			1	L
Townsend's solitaire[c]			1	T
Swainson's thrush	2	1.8	3	L
American robin	8	7.0	4	L
Varied thrush	4	3.5	4	B
Gray catbird	1	0.9	2	T
European starling[c]			1	T
Cedar waxwing	7	6.1	4	L
Nashville warbler[c]			1	T
Yellow warbler[c]			1	B
Yellow-rumped warbler	7	6.1	4	B
Townsend's warbler[c]			1	L
MacGillivray's warbler[c]			1	L
Wilson's warbler[c]			1	T
Western tanager	5	4.4	4	L
Spotted towhee[c]			1	T
Chipping sparrow	1	0.9	2	B
Fox sparrow	3	2.6	3	L
Song sparrow	5	4.4	4	L
Lincoln's sparrow	4	3.5	3	T
White-crowned sparrow	1	0.9	2	T
Dark-eyed junco	7	6.1	4	B
Red crossbill	11	9.6	4	L
Pine siskin	6	5.3	4	L
Evening grosbeak	1	0.9	2	T

[a] Total number recorded and percent of total based on unlimited distance point counts.
[b] B = Breeder; L = Likely Breeder; T = Transient; M = Migrant.
[c] Encountered outside of point counts.

Table 5. Relative abundances of 84 bird species at White Bird Battlefield, Idaho County, Idaho, from March 3, 1999 to September 17, 1999; 4 = abundant, 3 = common, 2 = uncommon or infrequent, 1 = rare; also shown are mean point count results and breeding status.

Species	Total #[a]	Birds/Count Period[a]	Density (Birds/ha)[a]	90% CI[a]	Total #[b]	% of Total[b]	Abundance Category	Breeding Status[c]
Pied-billed grebe[d]							1	M
Eared grebe	1	0.01			4	0.2	2	L
Great blue heron[d]							1	T
Turkey vulture[d]							1	T
Snow goose					1	0.1	2	M
Canada goose					133	7.2	4	M
Wood duck					2	0.1	2	L
American wigeon	1	0.01			1	0.1	2	L
Mallard	2	0.03	0.016	0.021	35	1.9	4	B
Blue-winged teal	3	0.04			27	1.5	3	B
Cinnamon teal	2	0.03			5	0.3	3	L
Northern shoveler					1	0.1	2	M
Green-winged teal					8	0.4	3	M
Redhead					2	0.1	2	M
Ring-necked duck	4	0.06	0.012	0.013	9	0.5	3	B
Bufflehead					4	0.2	2	M
Common goldeneye[d]							1	M
Barrow's goldeneye[d]							1	M
Ruddy duck	7	0.10	0.055	0.046	19	1.0	3	L
Bald eagle[d]							1	M
Northern harrier					2	0.1	2	T
Sharp-shinned hawk					1	0.1	2	T
Cooper's hawk					2	0.1	2	T
Red-tailed hawk					14	0.8	3	L
Golden eagle					6	0.3	3	B
American kestrel					12	0.7	3	L
Prairie falcon[d]							1	T
Chukar					27	1.5	3	L
Gray partridge	13	0.18	1.333	0.913	42	2.3	4	B
Ring-necked pheasant	1	0.01			39	2.1	4	L
California quail	3	0.04	0.011	0.012	71	3.9	4	L
Virginia rail[d]							1	M
Sora					5	0.3	3	M

Table 5. Relative abundances of 84 bird species at White Bird Battlefield, Idaho County, Idaho, from March 3, 1999 to September 17, 1999 (continued).

Species	Total #[a]	Birds/Count Period[a]	Density (Birds/ha)[a]	90% CI[a]	Total #[b]	% of total[b]	Abundance Category	Breeding Status[c]
American coot	94	1.31	0.290	0.362	279	15.1	4	L
Killdeer					13	0.7	3	L
Wilson's snipe					12	0.7	3	L
Wilson's phalarope					2	0.1	2	M
Rock pigeon	2	0.03	0.082	0.104	4	0.2	2	L
Mourning dove					13	0.7	3	L
Western screech-owl[d]							1	T
Great horned owl	1	0.01			2	0.1	2	T
Belted kingfisher[d]							1	L
Downy woodpecker					2	0.1	2	L
Hairy woodpecker					1	0.1	2	T
Northern flicker	1	0.01			18	1.0	3	L
Western wood-pewee	1	0.01			7	0.4	3	L
Willow flycatcher					1	0.1	2	T
Cordilleran flycatcher[d]							1	T
Say's phoebe[d]							1	T
Western kingbird[d]							1	T
Eastern kingbird	21	0.29	0.228	0.123	44	2.4	4	B
Warbling vireo	1	0.01			1	0.1	2	T
Red-eyed vireo	1	0.01			1	0.1	2	T
Black-billed magpie	5	0.07	0.027	0.024	95	5.2	4	L
Common raven					28	1.5	3	L
Violet-green swallow					87	4.7	4	L
Cliff swallow					14	0.8	3	T
Barn swallow					1	0.1	2	T
Black-capped chickadee					1	0.1	2	M
Rock wren	2	0.03	0.146	0.184	12	0.7	3	L
Canyon wren	2	0.03	0.016	0.021	5	0.3	3	L
House wren					3	0.2	2	T
American robin	2	0.03			13	0.7	3	L
European starling	9	0.13	0.339	0.249	114	6.2	4	L
Cedar waxwing					3	0.2	2	L
Yellow warbler	5	0.07	0.057	0.051	5	0.3	3	L
Yellow-rumped warbler					4	0.2	2	M
Yellow-breasted chat					6	0.3	3	L
Spotted Towhee					10	0.5	3	L

Table 5. Relative abundances of 84 bird species at White Bird Battlefield, Idaho County, Idaho, from March 3, 1999 to September 17, 1999 (continued)

Species	Total #[a]	Birds/Count Period[a]	Density (Birds/ha)[a]	90% CI[a]	Total #[b]	% of total[b]	Abundance Category	Breeding Status[c]
Chipping sparrow					1	0.1	1	T
Savannah sparrow	2	0.03	0.027	0.034	11	0.6	3	L
Grasshopper sparrow	1	0.01			1	0.1	1	T
Song sparrow	13	0.18	0.245	0.156	43	2.3	4	L
White-crowned sparrow					5	0.3	3	M
Dark-eyed junco[d]							1	M
Black-headed grosbeak					2	0.1	1	T
Lazuli bunting	20	0.28	1.962	1.044	51	2.8	4	L
Red-winged blackbird	20	0.28	0.123	0.087	88	4.8	4	B
Western meadowlark	43	0.60	0.341	0.147	204	11.1	4	B
Yellow-headed blackbird	13	0.18	0.053	0.043	42	2.3	4	B
Brewer's blackbird	5	0.07	0.046	0.043	41	2.2	4	B
Brown-headed cowbird	3	0.04	0.051	0.055	4	0.2	2	L
Bullock's oriole	18	0.25	0.112	0.063	28	1.5	3	B
American goldfinch	7	0.10	0.736	0.589	49	2.7	4	L

[a] Breeding season point count results (data truncated at 100 m). Sample sizes of one were too small for density analysis and were eliminated from the table.
[b] Total number recorded and percent of total based on unlimited distance point counts.
[c] B = Breeder; L = Likely Breeder; T = Transient; M = Migrant.
[d] Encountered outside of point counts.

Table 6. Relative abundances of 59 bird species at Old Chief Joseph Gravesite, Wallowa County, Oregon, from March 3, 1999 to December 21, 1999; 4 = abundant, 3 = common, 2 = uncommon or infrequent, 1 = rare; also shown are mean point count results and breeding status.

Species	Total #[a]	Birds/Count Period[a]	Density (Birds/ha)[a]	90% CI[a]	Total #[b]	% of total[b]	Abundance Category	Breeding Status[c]
Horned grebe[d]							3	M
Canada goose					70	53.8	4	T
Mallard[d]							3	T
Common goldeneye[d]							3	M
Common merganser[d]							3	M
Osprey[d]							3	T
Sharp-shinned hawk[d]							3	T
Cooper's hawk[d]							3	T
Swainson's hawk[d]							3	T
Red-tailed hawk					1	0.8	4	T
Rough-legged hawk[d]							2	M
Golden eagle					1	0.8	3	T
American kestrel[d]							2	L
California quail					1	0.8	3	T
Killdeer[d]							2	T
Great horned owl					2	1.5	4	T
Vaux's swift[d]							2	T
Calliope hummingbird[d]							2	T
Belted kingfisher[d]							2	T
Red-naped sapsucker[d]							2	T
Northern flicker	1	1.00			3	2.3	4	B
Western wood-pewee					2	1.5	4	L
Hammond's flycatcher	1	1.00			1	0.8	3	L
Warbling vireo					1	0.8	3	T
Clark's \nutcracker[d]							2	T
Black-billed magpie[d]							2	T
Common raven[d]							2	T
Tree swallow[d]							2	T
Violet-green swallow[d]							2	T
Northern rough-winged swallow[d]							2	T
Black-capped chickadee[d]							2	M
Red-breasted nuthatch[d]							2	M
Brown creeper[d]							2	M

Table 6. Relative abundances of 59 bird species at Old Chief Joseph Gravesite, Wallowa County, Oregon, from March 3, 1999 to December 21, 1999 (continued).

Species	Total #[a]	Birds/Count Period[a]	Density (Birds/ha)[a]	90% CI[a]	Total #[b]	% of total[b]	Abundance Category	Breeding Status[c]
House wren[d]							2	T
Winter wren[d]							2	M
American dipper[d]							1	T
Golden-crowned kinglet[d]							1	M
Mountain bluebird[d]							1	T
Townsend's solitaire[d]							1	M
Swainson's thrush[d]							1	M
American robin	1	1.00			8	6.2	4	B
European starling[d]							1	T
Cedar waxwing					22	16.9	4	T
Yellow warbler[d]							1	T
Yellow-rumped warbler	1	1.00			2	1.5	4	L
MacGillivray's warbler					1	0.8	3	L
Western tanager					1	0.8	3	T
Spotted towhee[d]							1	T
Chipping sparrow	2	2.00			2	1.5	4	L
White-crowned sparrow[d]							1	M
Lazuli bunting					2	1.5	4	T
Western meadowlark	1	1.00			1	0.8	3	L
Brewer's blackbird					1	0.8	3	L
Brown-headed cowbird	1	1.00			2	1.5	4	L
Gray-crowned rosy-finch[d]							1	M
House finch[d]							1	L
Red crossbill					1	0.8	3	T
Pine siskin					5	3.8	4	L
American goldfinch[d]							1	L

[a] Breeding season point count results (data truncated at 100 m). Sample sizes of one were too small for density analysis and were eliminated from the table.
[b] Total number recorded and percent of total based on unlimited distance point counts.
[c] B = Breeder; L = Likely Breeder; T = Transient; M = Migrant.
[d] Encountered outside of point counts.

Table 7. Relative abundances of 53 bird species at Bear Paw Battlefield, Blaine County, Montana, from February 6, 1999 to December 14, 1999; 4 = abundant, 3 = common, 2 = uncommon or infrequent, 1 = rare; also shown are mean point count results and breeding status.

Species	Total #[a]	Birds/Count Period[a]	Density (Birds/ha)[a]	90% CI[a]	Total #[b]	% of total[b]	Abundance Category	Breeding Status[c]
American white pelican					2	0.4	2	M
Great blue heron					2	0.4	2	T
Canada goose					7	1.3	3	T
American wigeon					6	1.1	3	M
Mallard					22	4.2	4	L
Northern shoveler					1	0.2	2	M
Northern pintail					1	0.2	2	M
Bald eagle					1	0.2	2	M
Northern harrier	4	0.13	0.135	0.136	41	7.8	4	B
Red-tailed hawk[d]							1	T
Ferruginous hawk					5	0.9	2	B
Golden eagle[d]							1	T
Prairie falcon					1	0.2	2	M
Ring-necked pheasant					39	7.4	4	B
Sandhill crane					5	0.9	2	T
Killdeer[d]							1	T
Willet					4	0.8	2	M
Long-billed curlew					5	0.9	2	T
Wilson's snipe	1	0.03			7	1.3	3	T
Franklin's gull					2	0.4	2	M
California gull					8	1.5	3	M
Rock pigeon					41	7.8	4	B
Mourning dove	3	0.10	0.018	0.021	4	0.8	2	L
Great horned owl[d]							1	T
Short-eared owl					1	0.2	2	T
Hairy woodpecker[d]							1	M
Willow flycatcher	3	0.10	0.027	0.030	14	2.7	3	T
Eastern kingbird	9	0.30	0.091	0.069	20	3.8	4	B
Black-billed magpie					6	1.1	3	L
American crow					1	0.2	2	T
Horned lark[d]							1	T
Cliff swallow	8	0.27	0.056	0.055	24	4.6	4	T
Barn swallow					12	2.3	3	T

Table 7. Relative abundances of 53 bird species at Bear Paw Battlefield, Blaine County, Montana, from February 6, 1999 to December 14, 1999 (continued).

Species	Total #[a]	Birds/Count Period[a]	Density (Birds/ha)[a]	90% CI[a]	Total #[b]	% of total[b]	Abundance Category	Breeding Status[c]
Black-capped chickadee[d]							1	M
Rock wren					1	0.2	2	M
House wren[d]							1	T
Ruby-crowned kinglet					1	0.2	1	M
American robin	1	0.03			6	1.1	3	T
Gray catbird	2	0.07	0.014	0.018	5	0.9	2	L
Sprague's pipit	3	0.10	0.035	0.039	25	4.7	4	B
Yellow warbler	3	0.10	0.042	0.046	14	2.7	3	B
Common yellowthroat	5	0.17	0.309	0.288	17	3.2	4	B
Wilson's warbler[d]							1	M
Spotted towhee	1	0.03			3	0.6	2	T
Clay-colored sparrow	24	0.80	5.522	3.269	42	8.0	4	B
Vesper sparrow	5	0.17	0.092	0.084	16	3.0	3	B
Savannah sparrow	4	0.13	0.071	0.072	10	1.9	3	B
Baird's sparrow	1	0.03			1	0.2	1	L
Song sparrow	2	0.07			12	2.3	3	B
Red-winged blackbird	2	0.07	0.126	0.162	24	4.6	4	B
Western meadowlark	12	0.40	0.221	0.150	43	8.2	4	L
Brown-headed cowbird	5	0.17	0.077	0.077	11	2.1	3	T
American goldfinch	1	0.03			14	2.7	3	L

[a] Breeding season point count results (data truncated at 100 m). Sample sizes of one were too small for density analysis and were eliminated from the table.
[b] Total number recorded and percent of total based on unlimited distance point counts.
[c] B = Breeder; L = Likely Breeder; T = Transient; M = Migrant.
[d] Encountered outside of point counts.

Table 8. Relative abundances of 83 bird species at Big Hole National Battlefield, Beaverhead County, Montana, from February 4, 1999 to December 16, 1999; 4 = abundant, 3 = common, 2 = uncommon or infrequent, 1 = rare; also shown are mean point count results and breeding status.

Species	Total #	Birds/Count Period[a]	Density (Birds/ha)[a]	90% CI[a]	Total #[b]	% of total[b]	Abundance Category	Breeding Status[c]
Great blue heron					1	0.2	2	T
Turkey vulture					1	0.2	2	T
Canada goose					12	2.0	4	T
American wigeon					12	2.0	4	M
Mallard					25	4.1	4	L
Northern pintail[d]							1	M
Green-winged teal					8	1.3	3	M
Bald eagle					1	0.2	2	M
Northern harrier					4	0.7	2	T
Cooper's hawk					1	0.2	2	T
Swainson's hawk					3	0.5	2	L
Red-tailed hawk					1	0.2	2	T
Rough-legged hawk					1	0.2	2	M
American kestrel					7	1.2	3	T
Prairie falcon[d]							1	M
Ruffed grouse	1	0.03			3	0.5	2	L
Sandhill crane	4	0.14	0.040	0.041	32	5.3	4	L
Killdeer					7	1.2	3	L
Spotted sandpiper	1	0.03			6	1.0	3	B
Wilson's snipe	1	0.03			28	4.6	4	L
Wilson's phalarope					6	1.0	3	M
Mourning dove					1	0.2	2	M
Great horned owl[d]							1	T
Northern pygmy-owl[d]							1	M
Long-eared owl[d]							1	T
Rufous hummingbird[d]							1	M
Belted kingfisher					6	1.0	3	L
Red-naped sapsucker	1	0.03			4	0.7	2	L
Downy woodpecker[d]							1	M
Northern flicker					17	2.8	4	B
Western wood-pewee	2	0.07			4	0.7	2	L
Willow flycatcher	2	0.07			6	1.0	3	L
Hammond's flycatcher[d]							1	T

Table 8. Relative abundances of 83 bird species at Big Hole National Battlefield, Beaverhead County, Montana, from February 4, 1999 to December 16, 1999 (continued).

Species	Total #	Birds/Count Period[a]	Density (Birds/ha)[a]	90% CI[a]	Total #[b]	% of total[b]	Abundance Category	Breeding Status[c]
Dusky flycatcher	6	0.21	0.062	0.053	11	1.8	3	B
Say's phoebe[d]							1	T
Eastern kingbird	1	0.03			8	1.3	3	B
Cassin's vireo	2	0.07	0.033	0.042	3	0.5	2	L
Warbling vireo	9	0.31	0.585	0.429	14	2.3	4	L
Gray jay					1	0.2	2	T
Clark's nutcracker					18	3.0	4	B
Black-billed magpie					1	0.2	2	T
American crow					4	0.7	2	T
Common raven					8	1.3	3	B
Tree swallow					3	0.5	2	T
Cliff swallow					18	3.0	4	T
Barn swallow[d]							1	T
Black-capped chickadee[d]							1	M
Mountain chickadee	4	0.14	0.074	0.073	14	2.3	4	B
Red-breasted nuthatch	2	0.07	0.017	0.021	5	0.8	3	L
House wren					1	0.2	1	T
American dipper[d]							1	L
Golden-crowned kinglet					5	0.8	3	M
Ruby-crowned kinglet	4	0.14	0.089	0.091	7	1.2	3	B
Mountain bluebird	1	0.03			3	0.5	2	L
Townsend's solitaire					1	0.2	1	T
Veery	1	0.03			4	0.7	2	B
Hermit thrush	2	0.07			3	0.5	2	T
American robin	13	0.45	3.309	2.252	45	7.5	4	B
Gray catbird					1	0.2	1	L
European starling					5	0.8	3	T
Yellow warbler	19	0.66	0.419	0.260	27	4.5	4	B
Yellow-rumped warbler	1	0.03			4	0.7	2	B
Northern waterthrush	6	0.21	0.083	0.071	12	2.0	4	B
Western tanager	1	0.03			5	0.8	3	T
American tree sparrow					4	0.7	2	M
Chipping sparrow	2	0.07	0.023	0.029	3	0.5	2	B
Brewer's sparrow	4	0.14	0.110	0.112	6	1.0	3	B
Vesper sparrow	10	0.34	0.104	0.077	12	2.0	3	B
Savannah sparrow	6	0.21	0.389	0.360	10	1.7	3	L

Table 8. Relative abundances of 83 bird species at Big Hole National Battlefield, Beaverhead County, Montana, from February 4, 1999 to December 16, 1999 (continued).

Species	Total #[a]	Birds/Count Period[a]	Density (Birds/ha)[a]	90% CI[a]	Total #[b]	% of total[b]	Abundance Category	Breeding Status[c]
Fox sparrow					3	0.5	2	L
Song sparrow	1	0.03			3	0.5	2	B
Lincoln's sparrow	1	0.03			3	0.5	2	T
White-crowned sparrow	4	0.14	0.040	0.039	7	1.2	3	B
Dark-eyed junco	5	0.17	0.080	0.073	20	3.3	4	B
Red-winged blackbird	3	0.10	0.032	0.036	20	3.3	4	L
Western meadowlark					3	0.5	2	T
Yellow-headed blackbird[d]							1	M
Brewer's blackbird	2	0.07	0.362	0.465	21	3.5	4	B
Brown-headed cowbird	3	0.10			5	0.8	3	L
Cassin's finch					2	0.3	2	L
Red crossbill					9	1.5	3	M
Common redpoll[d]							1	M
Pine siskin					34	5.6	4	L

[a] Breeding season point count results (data truncated at 100 m). Sample sizes of one were too small for density analysis and were eliminated from the table.
[b] Total number recorded and percent of total based on unlimited distance point counts.
[c] B = Breeder; L = Likely Breeder; T = Transient; M = Migrant.
[d] Encountered outside of point counts.

Table 9. Relative abundances of 25 bird species at Whitman Mission National Historic Site, Walla Walla County, Washington, July 15, 2001; 4 = abundant, 3 = common, 2 = uncommon or infrequent, 1 = rare.

Species	# recorded	% of total	Abundance category
Wood duck	1	1.2	1
Northern harrier	1	1.2	1
Sharp-shinned hawk	1	1.2	1
Swainson's hawk	2	2.3	2
American kestrel	3	3.5	3
Ring-billed gull	11	12.8	4
Mourning dove	1	1.2	1
Downy woodpecker	1	1.2	1
Northern flicker	2	2.3	2
Western wood-pewee	1	1.2	1
Black-billed magpie	1	1.2	2
American crow	13	15.1	4
Northern rough-winged swallow	16	18.6	4
Barn swallow	3	3.5	3
Bewick's wren	2	2.3	2
House wren	1	1.2	2
American robin	7	8.1	4
European starling	3	3.5	3
Song sparrow	4	4.7	3
Black-headed grosbeak	2	2.3	3
Red-winged blackbird	4	4.7	4
Brown-headed cowbird	2	2.3	3
House finch	2	2.3	3
American goldfinch	1	1.2	2
Unidentified hummingbird	1	1.2	2

Table 10. Plant species identified within vegetation releves at Buffalo Eddy, Asotin County, Washington.

Common Name	Scientific Name
American vetch	*Vicia americana*
Arrowleaf balsamroot	*Balsamorhiza sagittata*
Blue elderberry	*Sambucus cerulea*
Bluebunch wheatgrass	*Elytrigia spicata* (prev. *Agropyron spicatum*)
Cheatgrass	*Bromus tectorum*
Chicory	*Cichorium intybus*
Clematis	*Clematis* sp.
Common mullein	*Verbascum thapsus*
Common St. John's wort	*Hypericum perforatum*
Common yarrow	*Achillea millefolium*
Hackberry	*Celtis reticulata*
Houndstongue	*Cynoglossum officinale*
Mint	*Mentha* sp.
Moss	
Moth mullein	*Verbascum blattaria*
Mulberry	*Morus alba*
Poison ivy	*Rhus radicans*
Rabbit-brush	*Chrysothamnus* sp.
Scotch thistle	*Onopordum acanthium*
Serviceberry	*Amelanchier alnifolia*
Smooth sumac	*Rhus glabra*
Syringa	*Philadelphus lewisii*
Thistle	*Cirsium* sp.
Western salsify	*Tragopogon dubius*
Yellow star-thistle	*Centaurea solstitialis*

Table 11. Plant species identified within vegetation releves at Spalding, Nez Perce County, Idaho.

Common Name	Scientific Name
Ash	*Fraxinus* sp.
Black cottonwood	*Populus trichocarpa*
Black locust	*Robinia pseudo-acacia*
Blue elderberry	*Sambucus cerulea*
Bluebunch wheatgrass	*Elytrigia spicata* (prev. *Agropyron spicatum*)
Buckhorn plantain	*Plantago lanceolata*
California brome	*Bromus carinatus*
Chicory	*Cichorium intybus*
Cinquefoil	*Potentilla gracilis*
Common cattail	*Typha latifolia*
Common chokecherry	*Prunus virginiana*
Common cocklebur	*Xanthium strumarium*
Common mullein	*Verbascum thapsus*
Common tansy	*Tanacetum vulgare*
Common teasel	*Dipsacus fullonum*
Curly dock	*Rumex crispus*
Dogbane	*Apocynum* sp.
Dwarf mallow	*Malva neglecta*
Field bindweed	*Convolvulus arvensis*
Hackberry	*Celtis reticulata*
Himalayan blackberry	*Rubus discolor*
Hop	*Humulus lupulus*
Italian ryegrass	*Lolium multiflorum*
Japanese knotweed	*Polygonum cuspidatum*
Johnsongrass	*Sorghum halepense*
Lilac	*Syringa vulgaris*
Maple	*Acer* sp.
Matrimony vine	*Lycium halimifolium*
Moss	
Mulberry	*Morus alba*
Nuttall's Sego lily	*Calochortus nuttallii*
Pearhip rose	*Rosa woodsii*
Poison hemlock	*Conium maculatum*
Ponderosa pine	*Pinus ponderosa*
Prickly lettuce	*Lactuca serriola*
Prostrate knotweed	*Polygonum aviculare*
Reed canarygrass	*Phalaris arundinacea*
Rose species	*Rosa* sp.
Ryegrass	*Lolium* sp.

Table 11. Plant species identified within vegetation releves at Spalding, Nez Perce County, Idaho (continued).

Common Name	Scientific Name
Serviceberry	*Amelanchier alnifolia*
Smooth sumac	*Rhus glabra*
Spotted knapweed	*Centaurea maculosa*
Sycamore	*Platanus* sp.
Syringa	*Philadelphus lewisii*
Tall Oregon grape	*Berberis aquifolium*
Unidentified pine	*Pinus* sp.
Western clematis	*Clematis ligusticifolia*
Western wildcucumber	*Marah oreganus*
White horehound	*Marrubium vulgare*
White poplar	*Populus alba*
Wild oat	*Avena fatua*
Willow	*Salix* sp.
Witchgrass	*Panicum capillare*
Yellow star-thistle	*Centaurea solstitialis*

Table 12. Plant species identified within vegetation releves at Heart of the Monster, Idaho County, Idaho.

Common Name	Scientific Name
Bittersweet nightshade	*Solanum dulcamara*
Black cottonwood	*Populus trichocarpa*
Black hawthorn	*Crataegus douglasii*
Black locust	*Robinia pseudo-acacia*
Bracken fern	*Pteridium aquilinum*
Buckhorn plantain	*Plantago lanceolata*
Bull thistle	*Cirsium vulgare*
Canada goldenrod	*Solidago canadensis*
Canada thistle	*Cirsium arvense*
Cascara	*Rhamnus purshiana*
Common chokecherry	*Prunus virginiana*
Common mullein	*Verbascum thapsus*
Common snowberry	*Symphoricarpos albus*
Common St. John's wort	*Hypericum perforatum*
Common teasel	*Dipsacus fullonum*
Common yarrow	*Achillea millefolium*
Curly dock	*Rumex crispus*
Field bindweed	*Convolvulus arvensis*
Field pennycress	*Thlaspi arvense*
Hairy vetch	*Vicia villosa*
Himalayan blackberry	*Rubus discolor*
Lilac	*Syringa vulgaris*
Mint	*Mentha* sp.
Moss	
Moth mullein	*Verbascum blattaria*
Oxeye daisy	*Chrysanthemum leucanthemum*
Queen Anne's lace	*Daucus carota*
Reed canarygrass	*Phalaris arundinacea*
Serviceberry	*Amelanchier alnifolia*
Spotted knapweed	*Centaurea maculosa*
Syringa	*Philadelphus lewisii*
Timothy	*Phleum pratense*
Western salsify	*Tragopogon dubius*
Western thimbleberry	*Rubus parviflorus*
White campion	*Silene alba*
White clover	*Melilotus* sp.
Witchgrass	*Panicum capillare*
Yellow sweetclover	*Melilotus officinalis*

Table 13. Plant species identified within vegetation releves along the Lolo Trail and Lolo Pass/Musselshell Meadow, Clearwater and Idaho Counties, Idaho.

Common Name	Scientific Name
Alpine knotweed	*Polygonum phytolaccaefolium*
Alpine mitrewort	*Mitella pentandra*
American false hellebore	*Veratrum viride*
Arrowleaf groundsel	*Senecio triangularis*
Aster	*Aster* sp.
Baldhip rose	*Rosa gymnocarpa*
Baneberry	*Actaea rubra*
Bearberry honeysuckle	*Lonicera involucrata*
Beargrass	*Xerophyllum tenax*
Big huckleberry	*Vaccinium membranaceum*
Black hawthorn	*Crataegus douglasii*
Blue wildrye	*Elymus glaucus*
Bluejoint reedgrass	*Calamagrostis canadensis*
Bracken fern	*Pteridium aquilinum*
Bracted lousewort	*Pedicularis bracteosa*
Bull thistle	*Cirsium vulgare*
Bunchberry	*Cornus canadensis*
Buttercup	*Ranunculus* sp.
California false hellebore	*Veratrum californicum*
Canada goldenrod	*Solidago canadensis*
Cinquefoil	*Potentilla gracilis*
Cinquefoil	*Potentilla* sp.
Common camas	*Camassia quamash*
Common mullein	*Verbascum thapsus*
Common snowberry	*Symphoricarpos albus*
Common St. John's wort	*Hypericum perforatum*
Common yarrow	*Achillea millefolium*
Coolwort foamflower	*Tiarella trifoliata*
Cow parsnip	*Heracleum lanatum*
Desert phlox	*Phlox austromontana*
Dogtooth violet	*Erythronium grandiflorum*
Douglas-fir	*Pseudotsuga menziesii*
Dwarf bilberry	*Vaccinium myrtillus*
Elderberry	*Sambucus racemosa*
Elephant's head	*Pedicularis groenlandica*
Elk sedge	*Carex geyeri*
Engelmann spruce	*Picea engelmannii*
False bugbane	*Trautvetteria caroliniensis*
False Solomon's seal	*Smilacina racemosa*
Field horsetail	*Equisetum arvense*

Table 13. Plant species identified within vegetation releves along the Lolo Trail and Lolo Pass/Musselshell Meadow, Clearwater and Idaho Counties, Idaho (continued).

Common Name	Scientific Name
Field woodrush	*Luzula campestris*
Fireweed	*Epilobium angustifolium*
Fool's huckleberry	*Menziesia ferruginea*
Goldenrod	*Solidago* sp.
Grand fir	*Abies grandis*
Grouse whortleberry	*Vaccinium scoparium*
Harebell	*Campanula* sp.
Houndstongue	*Cynoglossum officinale*
Huckleberry	*Vaccinium* sp.
Indian paintbrush	*Castilleja* sp.
Jacob's ladder	*Polemonium pulcherrimum*
Kentucky bluegrass	*Poa pratensis*
Labrador tea	*Ledum glandulosum*
Ladyfern	*Athyrium filix-femina*
Leafy lousewort	*Pedicularis racemosa*
Leafy thistle	*Cirsium foliosum*
Lodgepole pine	*Pinus contorta*
Lupine	*Lupinus* sp.
Maidenhair fern	*Adiantum pedatum*
Mimulus	*Mimulus* sp.
Montana golden pea	*Thermopsis montana*
Moss	
Mountain alder	*Alnus incana*
Mountain arnica	*Arnica latifolia*
Mountain boykinia	*Boykinia major*
Mountain hemlock	*Tsuga mertensiana*
Mountain-ash	*Sorbus scopulina*
Needle-and-thread	*Stipa comata*
Needlegrass	*Stipa* sp.
Northwestern sedge	*Carex concinnoides*
Oak-fern	*Gymnocarpium dryopteris*
Ocean-spray	*Holodiscus discolor*
One-sided wintergreen	*Pyrola secunda*
Pachistima	*Pachistima myrsinites*
Pathfinder	*Adenocaulon bicolor*
Pearhip rose	*Rosa woodsii*
Pearly everlasting	*Anaphalis margaritacea*
Penstemon	*Penstemon* sp.
Pinegrass	*Calamagrostis rubescens*
Prince's-pine	*Chimaphila umbellata*

Table 13. Plant species identified within vegetation releves along the Lolo Trail and Lolo Pass/Musselshell Meadow, Clearwater and Idaho Counties, Idaho (continued).

Common Name	Scientific Name
Queen Anne's lace	*Daucus carota*
Queen cup beadlily	*Clintonia uniflora*
Red columbine	*Aquilegia formosa*
Red mountain-heather	*Phyllodoce empetriformis*
Red raspberry	*Rubus idaeus*
Red-osier dogwood	*Cornus stolonifera*
Rein-orchid	*Habenaria sp.*
Rocky Mountain maple	*Acer glabrum*
Ross sedge	*Carex rossii*
Round-leaved violet	*Viola orbiculata*
Rudbeckia	*Rudbeckia occidentalis*
Rush	*Juncus* sp.
Scouler willow	*Salix scouleriana*
Sedge	*Carex* sp.
Self-heal	*Prunella vulgaris*
Serviceberry	*Amelanchier alnifolia*
Showy aster	*Aster conspicuus*
Side-flowered mitrewort	*Mitella stauropetala*
Sitka alder	*Alnus sinuata*
Sitka valerian	*Valeriana stichensis*
Smooth sumac	*Rhus glabra*
Smooth woodrush	*Luzula hitchcockii*
Spotted knapweed	*Centaurea maculosa*
Starry Solomon-seal	*Smilacina stellata*
Sticky cinquefoil	*Potentilla glandulosa*
Stinging nettle	*Urtica dioica*
Strawberry	*Fragaria virginiana*
Subalpine fir	*Abies lasiocarpa*
Subalpine spiraea	*Spiraea densiflora*
Sweetscented bedstraw	*Galium triflorum*
Tall bluebells	*Mertensia paniculata*
Tall mountain shooting star	*Dodecatheon jeffreyi*
Timothy	*Phleum pratense*
Tiny-bloom penstemon	*Penstemon procerus*
Trillium	*Trillium ovatum*
Twinflower	*Linnaea borealis*
Utah honeysuckle	*Lonicera utahensis*
Verticillate-umbel licorice-root	*Ligusticum verticillatum*
Western goldthread	*Coptis occidentalis*
Western hemlock	*Tsuga heterophylla*

Table 13. Plant species identified within vegetation releves along the Lolo Trail and Lolo Pass/Musselshell Meadow, Clearwater and Idaho Counties, Idaho (continued).

Common Name	Scientific Name
Western larch	*Larix occidentalis*
Western meadowrue	*Thalictrum occidentale*
Western rattlesnake-plantain	*Goodyera oblongifolia*
Western red cedar	*Thuja plicata*
Western thimbleberry	*Rubus parviflorus*
Western wintergreen	*Gaultheria humifusa*
Western yew	*Taxus brevifolia*
White coiled-beak lousewort	*Pedicularis contorta*
White pine	*Pinus monticola*
White rhododendron	*Rhododendron albiflorum*
White-flowered hawkweed	*Hieracium albiflorum*
Wild ginger	*Asarum caudatum*
Windflower	*Anemone piperi*
Woods strawberry	*Fragaria vesca*

Table 14. Plant species identified within vegetation releves at White Bird Battlefield, Idaho County, Idaho.

Common Name	Scientific Name
Common yarrow	*Achillea millefolium*
Threeawn	*Aristida longiseta*
Mustard	*Brassica* sp.
Smallseed falseflax	*Camelina microcarpa*
Hackberry	*Celtis reticulata*
Yellow star-thistle	*Centaurea solstitialis*
Canada thistle	*Cirsium arvense*
Chicory	*Cichorium intybus*
Western clematis	*Clematis ligusticifolia*
Field bindweed	*Convolvulus arvensis*
Black hawthorn	*Crataegus douglasii*
Houndstongue	*Cynoglossum officinale*
Queen Anne's lace	*Daucus carota*
Common teasel	*Dipsacus fullonum*
Ash	*Fraxinus* sp.
Catchweed bedstraw	*Galium aparine*
Common sunflower	*Helianthus annuus*
Common St. John's wort	*Hypericum perforatum*
Prickly lettuce	*Lactuca serriola*
Clasping pepperweed	*Lepidium perfoliatum*
Italian ryegrass	*Lolium multiflorum*
Lupine	*Lupinus* sp.
Matrimony vine	*Lycium halimifolium*
Dwarf mallow	*Malva neglecta*
White horehound	*Marrubium vulgare*
Moss	
Catnip	*Nepeta cataria*
Scotch thistle	*Onopordum acanthium*
Reed canarygrass	*Phalaris arundinacea*
Plum	*Prunus* sp.
Black cottonwood	*Populus trichocarpa*
Cherry, Plum	*Prunus* sp.
Cultivated apple	*Pyrus malus*
Smooth sumac	*Rhus glabra*
Poison ivy	*Rhus radicans*
Currant	*Ribes* sp.
Dog rose	*Rosa canina*
Curly dock	*Rumex crispus*
Blue elderberry	*Sambucus cerulea*
Bulrush	*Scirpus* sp.

Table 14. Plant species identified within vegetation releves at White Bird Battlefield, Idaho County, Idaho (continued).

Common Name	Scientific Name
Tumblemustard; Jim Hill mustard	*Sisymbrium altissimum*
Lilac	*Syringa vulgaris*
Field pennycress	*Thlaspi arvense*
Common cattail	*Typha latifolia*
Moth mullein	*Verbascum blattaria*
Common mullein	*Verbascum thapsus*
Hairy vetch	*Vicia villosa*
Common cocklebur	*Xanthium strumarium*

Table 15. Plant species identified within vegetation releves at Old Chief Joseph Gravesite, Wallowa County, Oregon.

Common Name	Scientific Name
Artemisia	*Artemisia* sp.
Baldhip rose	*Rosa gymnocarpa*
Beckmannia	*Beckmannia syzigachne*
Black hawthorn	*Crataegus douglasii*
Bluebunch wheatgrass	*Elytrigia spicata* (prev. *Agropyron spicatum*)
California false hellebore	*Veratrum californicum*
Cheatgrass	*Bromus tectorum*
Cinquefoil	*Potentilla* sp.
Common chokecherry	*Prunus virginiana*
Common mallow	*Malva sylvestris*
Common mullein	*Verbascum thapsus*
Common snowberry	*Symphoricarpos albus*
Common yarrow	*Achillea millefolium*
Creeping Oregon grape	*Berberis repens*
Douglas rabbitbrush	*Chrysothamnus viscidiflorus*
Eriogonum	*Eriogonum* sp.
Goldenrod	*Solidago* sp.
Gromwell	*Lithospermum* sp.
Houndstongue	*Cynoglossum officinale*
Idaho fescue	*Festuca idahoensis*
Junegrass	*Koeleria nitida* (prev. *Koeleria cristata*)
Lomatium	*Lomatium* sp.
Lupine	*Lupinus* sp.
Meadow salsify	*Tragopogon pratensis*
Moss	
Mustard	*Brassica* sp.
Ponderosa pine	*Pinus ponderosa*
Reed canarygrass	*Phalaris arundinacea*
Sego lily	*Calochortus* sp.
Serviceberry	*Amelanchier alnifolia*
Showy aster	*Aster conspicuus*
Sticky purple geranium	*Geranium viscosissimum*
Wax currant	*Ribes cereum*
White-flowered hawkweed	*Hieracium albiflorum*

Table 16. Plant species identified within vegetation releves at Bear Paw Battlefield, Blaine County, Montana.

Common Name	Scientific Name
Artemisia	*Artemisia* sp.
Aster	*Aster* sp.
Beckmannia	*Beckmannia syzigachne*
Big sagebrush	*Artemisia tridentata*
Blue grama	*Bouteloua gracilis*
Bluebunch wheatgrass	*Elytrigia spicata* (prev. *Agropyron spicatum*)
Bull thistle	*Cirsium vulgare*
Common snowberry	*Symphoricarpos albus*
Common yarrow	*Achillea millefolium*
Coneflower	*Ratibida columnifera*
Gaillardia	*Gaillardia aristata*
Goldenrod	*Solidago* sp.
Horsetail	*Equisetum* sp.
Lupine	*Lupinus* sp.
Milkweed	*Asclepias* sp.
Moss	
Mustard	*Brassica* sp.
Needle-and-thread	*Stipa comata*
Pearhip rose	*Rosa woodsii*
Prickly-pear cactus	*Opuntia polycantha*
Rabbit-brush	*Chrysothamnus* sp.
Red-osier dogwood	*Cornus stolonifera*
Reed canarygrass	*Phalaris arundinacea*
Rush	*Juncus* sp.
Saltgrass	*Distichlis stricta*
Sedge	*Carex* sp.
Spotted knapweed	*Centaurea maculosa*
Unidentified composite	
Unidentified grass	
Western salsify	*Tragopogon dubius*
White clover	*Melilotus* sp.
Wild licorice	*Glycyrrhiza lepidota*
Willow	*Salix* sp.
Yellow sweetclover	*Melilotus officinalis*

Table 17. Plant species identified within vegetation releves at Big Hole National Battlefield, Beaverhead County, Montana.

Common Name	Scientific Name
American bistort	*Polygonum bistortoides*
Arrowleaf balsamroot	*Balsamorhiza sagittata*
Baltic rush	*Juncus balticus*
Bearded wheatgrass	*Agropyron caninum*
Bedstraw	*Galium* sp.
Big sagebrush	*Artemisia tridentata*
Black-hairy microseris	*Microseris nigrescens*
Blue huckleberry	*Vaccinium globulare*
Bluebells	*Mertensia viridis*
Bluebunch wheatgrass	*Elytrigia spicata* (prev. *Agropyron spicatum*)
Canada goldenrod	*Solidago canadensis*
Cinquefoil	*Potentilla gracilis*
Common camas	*Camassia quamash*
Common yarrow	*Achillea millefolium*
Creeping Oregon grape	*Berberis repens*
Cusick's paintbrush	*Castilleja cusickii*
Diverse-leaved cinquefoil	*Potentilla diversifolia*
Douglas rabbitbrush	*Chrysothamnus viscidiflorus*
Douglas-fir	*Pseudotsuga menziesii*
Douglas's sedge	*Carex douglasii*
Elk sedge	*Carex geyeri*
Fiddleneck	*Amsinckia* sp.
Field woodrush	*Luzula campestris*
Fireweed	*Epilobium angustifolium*
Frasera	*Frasera albicaulis*
Geranium	*Geranium* sp.
Geyer's onion	*Allium geyeri*
Grouse whortleberry	*Vaccinium scoparium*
Heartleaf arnica	*Arnica cordifolia*
Hook violet	*Viola adunca*
Houndstongue hawkweed	*Hieracium cynoglossoides*
Idaho fescue	*Festuca idahoensis*
Junegrass	*Koeleria nitida* (prev. *Koeleria cristata*)
Kentucky bluegrass	*Poa pratensis*
Lance-leaved sedum	*Sedum lanceolatum*
Leafy aster	*Aster foliaceus*
Leafy thistle	*Cirsium foliosum*
Lichen	
Liddon's sedge	*Carex petasata*
Lodgepole pine	*Pinus contorta*

Table 17. Plant species identified within vegetation releves at Big Hole National Battlefield, Beaverhead County, Montana (continued).

Common Name	Scientific Name
Long-leaf fleabane	*Erigeron corymbosus*
Long-leaf phlox	*Phlox longifolia*
Long-leaved aster	*Aster chilensis*
Long-leaved hawksbeard	*Crepis acuminata*
Long-plumed avens	*Geum triflorum*
Long-stalked clover	*Trifolium longipes*
Long-styled rush	*Juncus longistylis*
Meadow death-camas	*Zigadenus venenosus*
Montana goldenrod	*Solidago missouriensis*
Moss	
Nebraska sedge	*Carex nebraskensis*
Needle-and-thread	*Stipa comata*
Nine-leaved lomatium	*Lomatium triternatum*
Northern bedstraw	*Galium boreale*
Northwestern sedge	*Carex concinnoides*
Nuttall's Sego lily	*Calochortus nuttallii*
One-sided wintergreen	*Pyrola secunda*
Orange arnica	*Arnica fulgens*
Pearly everlasting	*Anaphalis margaritacea*
Pinegrass	*Calamagrostis rubescens*
Ponderosa pine	*Pinus ponderosa*
Prairie gentian	*Gentiana affinis*
Prince's-pine	*Chimaphila* sp.
Quaking aspen	*Populus tremuloides*
Queen Anne's lace	*Daucus carota*
Red-seeded dandelion	*Taraxacum laevigatum*
Rocky Mountain aster	*Aster stenomeres*
Ross sedge	*Carex rossii*
Rosy pussy-toes	*Antennaria microphylla*
Scarlet gilia	*Gilia aggregata*
Scouler willow	*Salix scouleriana*
Sedge	*Carex* sp.
Serviceberry	*Amelanchier alnifolia*
Showy fleabane	*Erigeron speciosus*
Shrubby cinquefoil	*Potentilla fruticosa*
Silver lupine	*Lupinus argenteus*
Slimpod shooting star	*Dodecatheon conjugens*
Smooth brome	*Bromus inermis*
Snowberry	*Symphoricarpos sp.*
Spiraea	*Spiraea betufolia*

Table 17. Plant species identified within vegetation releves at Big Hole National Battlefield, Beaverhead County, Montana (continued).

Common Name	Scientific Name
Strawberry	*Fragaria* sp.
Strawberry	*Fragaria virginiana*
Sulfurflower	*Eriogonum umbellatum*
Thin-leaved owl-clover	*Orthocarpus tenuifolius*
Thistle	*Cirsium* sp.
Thread-leaved sedge	*Carex filifolia*
Timber oatgrass	*Danthonia intermedia*
Timothy	*Phleum pratense*
Tiny-bloom penstemon	*Penstemon procerus*
Tufted hairgrass	*Deschampsia caespitosa*
Western gromwell	*Lithospermum ruderale*
Western groundsel	*Senecio integerrimus*
Western needlegrass	*Stipa occidentalis*
Western thimbleberry	*Rubus parviflorus*
White coiled-beak lousewort	*Pedicularis contorta*
Willow	*Salix* sp.
Wyeth lupine	*Lupinus wyethii*

Table 18. Ecological systems by site and point count station.

Site	Point	Ecological System
Buffalo Eddy	1	Columbia Basin Foothill and Canyon Dry Grassland
	2	Columbia Basin Foothill and Canyon Dry Grassland
	3	Columbia Basin Foothill and Canyon Dry Grassland
Spalding	1	Columbia Basin Foothill Riparian Woodland and Shrubland
	2	Developed--Arboretum
	3	Columbia Basin Foothill Riparian Woodland and Shrubland
	4	Disturbed and Invasive Grass and Forb
	5	Disturbed and Invasive Grass and Forb
	6	Developed
Heart of the Monster	1	Columbia Basin Foothill Riparian Woodland and Shrubland/Disturbed and Invasive Grass and Forb
	2	Columbia Basin Foothill Riparian Woodland and Shrubland/Disturbed and Invasive Grass and Forb
	3	Columbia Basin Foothill Riparian Woodland and Shrubland/Disturbed and Invasive Grass and Forb
	4	North American Arid West Emergent Marsh/Disturbed and Invasive Grass and Forb
Lolo Trail and Lolo Pass/Musselshell Meadow	1	Rocky Mountain Subalpine Dry-Mesic Spruce-Fir Forest and Woodland
	2	Northern Rocky Mountain Montane Mixed Conifer Forest
	3	Northern Rocky Mountain Montane Mixed Conifer Forest
	4	North Pacific Mountain Hemlock Forest
	5	Rocky Mountain Lodgepole Pine Forest
	6	North Pacific Mountain Hemlock Forest
	7	North Pacific Mountain Hemlock Forest
	8	Rocky Mountain Subalpine Dry-Mesic Spruce-Fir Forest and Woodland
	9	Rocky Mountain Lodgepole Pine Forest
	10	Rocky Mountain Subalpine Dry-Mesic Spruce-Fir Forest and Woodland
	11	Northern Rocky Mountain Montane Mixed Conifer Forest
	12	Rocky Mountain Subalpine Dry-Mesic Spruce-Fir Forest and Woodland
	13	Rocky Mountain Subalpine Dry-Mesic Spruce-Fir Forest and Woodland
	14	Northern Rocky Mountain Montane Mixed Conifer Forest
	15	Northern Rocky Mountain Western Red-cedar-Hemlock Forest
	16	Northern Rocky Mountain Montane Mixed Conifer Forest
White Bird Battlefield	1	Columbia Plateau Grassland and Steppe/Columbia Basin Foothill Riparian Woodland and Shrub
	2	Columbia Plateau Grassland and Steppe
	3	Columbia Plateau Grassland and Steppe/Hackberry Woodland
	4	Columbia Plateau Grassland and Steppe
	5	Columbia Plateau Grassland and Steppe
	6	Columbia Plateau Grassland and Steppe/Hackberry Woodland
	7	Columbia Plateau Grassland and Steppe
	8	Hackberry Woodland
	9	Columbia Plateau Grassland and Steppe
	10	Columbia Plateau Grassland and Steppe
	11	Columbia Plateau Grassland and Steppe
	12	Columbia Plateau Grassland and Steppe
	13	Columbia Plateau Grassland and Steppe
	14	Columbia Plateau Grassland and Steppe
	15	Columbia Plateau Grassland and Steppe
	16	Columbia Plateau Grassland and Steppe
	17	Columbia Plateau Grassland and Steppe
	18	Columbia Plateau Grassland and Steppe
	19	Columbia Plateau Grassland and Steppe
	20	Columbia Plateau Grassland and Steppe
	21	Columbia Plateau Grassland and Steppe/Hackberry Woodland

Table 18. Ecological systems by site and point count station (continued).

Site	Point	Ecological System
	22	Columbia Plateau Grassland and Steppe/Hackberry Woodland
	23	Columbia Plateau Grassland and Steppe/Hackberry Woodland
	24	Columbia Plateau Grassland and Steppe
Old Chief Joseph Gravesite	1	Rocky Mountain Ponderosa Pine Woodland
Bear Paw Battlefield	1	Disturbed-grassland
	2	Disturbed-grassland
	3	Disturbed-grassland
	4	Northwestern Great Plains Mixedgrass Prairie
	5	Western Great Plains Riparian Woodland and Shrubland
	6	Northwestern Great Plains Mixedgrass Prairie
	7	Northwestern Great Plains Mixedgrass Prairie
	8	Northwestern Great Plains Mixedgrass Prairie
	9	Northwestern Great Plains Mixedgrass Prairie
	10	Northwestern Great Plains Mixedgrass Prairie
Big Hole National Battlefield	1	Rocky Mountain Lodgepole Pine Forest
	2	Rocky Mountain Lodgepole Pine Forest
	3	Inter-Mountain Basins Montane Sagebrush Steppe
	4	Inter-Mountain Basins Montane Sagebrush Steppe
	5	Rocky Mountain Subalpine-Montane Riparian Shrubland
	6	Rocky Mountain Subalpine-Montane Riparian Shrubland
	7	Inter-Mountain Basins Montane Sagebrush Steppe
	8	Inter-Mountain Basins Montane Sagebrush Steppe
	11	Rocky Mountain Subalpine-Montane Riparian Shrubland
	12	Rocky Mountain Subalpine-Montane Riparian Shrubland

Appendix Families and common and scientific names for the 164 bird species detected in Nez Perce National Historical Park and Big Hole National Battlefield in 1999. Taxonomy follows the American Ornithologists' Union Check-list (American Ornithologists' Union 1998) and incorporates changes made in the 42nd, 43rd, 44th, and 45th Supplements to the Check-list, as published in *The Auk* 117: 847-858 (2000); 119:897-906 (2002); 120:923-931 (2003); 121:985-995 (2004).

Family Name	Common Name	Scientific Name
Anatidae	Snow goose	*Chen caerulescens*
	Canada goose	*Branta canadensis*
	Wood duck	*Aix sponsa*
	American wigeon	*Anas americana*
	Mallard	*Anas platyrhynchos*
	Blue-winged teal	*Anas discors*
	Cinnamon teal	*Anas cyanoptera*
	Northern shoveler	*Anas clypeata*
	Northern pintail	*Anas acuta*
	Green-winged teal	*Anas crecca*
	Redhead	*Aythya americana*
	Ring-necked duck	*Aythya collaris*
	Bufflehead	*Bucephala albeola*
	Common goldeneye	*Bucephala clangula*
	Barrow's goldeneye	*Bucephala islandica*
	Hooded merganser	*Lophodytes cucullatus*
	Common merganser	*Mergus merganser*
	Ruddy duck	*Oxyura jamaicensis*
Phasianidae	Chukar	*Alectoris chukar*
	Gray partridge	*Perdix perdix*
	Ring-necked pheasant	*Phasianus colchicus*
	Ruffed grouse	*Bonasa umbellus*
	Spruce grouse	*Falcipennis canadensis*
	Wild turkey	*Meleagris gallopavo*
Odontophoridae	California quail	*Callipepla californica*
Podicipedidae	Pied-billed grebe	*Podilymbus podiceps*
	Horned grebe	*Podiceps auritus*
	Eared grebe	*Podiceps nigricollis*
Pelecanidae	American white pelican	*Pelecanus erythrorhynchos*
Ardeidae	Great blue heron	*Ardea herodias*
Cathartidae	Turkey vulture	*Cathartes aura*
Accipitridae	Osprey	*Pandion haliaetus*
	Bald eagle	*Haliaeetus leucocephalus*
	Northern harrier	*Circus cyaneus*
	Sharp-shinned hawk	*Accipiter striatus*
	Cooper's hawk	*Accipiter cooperii*

Appendix Families and common and scientific names for the 164 bird species detected in Nez Perce National Historical Park and Big Hole National Battlefield in 1999 (continued).

Family Name	Common Name	Scientific Name
	Swainson's hawk	*Buteo swainsoni*
	Red-tailed hawk	*Buteo jamaicensis*
	Ferruginous hawk	*Buteo regalis*
	Rough-legged hawk	*Buteo lagopus*
	Golden eagle	*Aquila chrysaetos*
Falconidae	American kestrel	*Falco sparverius*
	Prairie falcon	*Falco mexicanus*
Rallidae	Virginia rail	*Rallus limicola*
	Sora	*Porzana carolina*
	American coot	*Fulica americana*
Gruidae	Sandhill crane	*Grus canadensis*
Charadriidae	Killdeer	*Charadrius vociferus*
Scolopacidae	Willet	*Catoptrophorus semipalmatus*
	Spotted sandpiper	*Actitis macularia*
	Long-billed curlew	*Numenius americanus*
	Wilson's snipe	*Gallinago delicata*
	Wilson's phalarope	*Phalaropus tricolor*
Laridae	Franklin's gull	*Larus pipixcan*
	Ring-billed gull	*Larus delawarensis*
	California gull	*Larus californicus*
Columbidae	Rock pigeon	*Columba livia*
	Mourning dove	*Zenaida macroura*
Tytonidae	Barn owl	*Tyto alba*
Strigidae	Western screech-owl	*Megascops kennicottii*
	Great horned owl	*Bubo virginianus*
	Northern pygmy-owl	*Glaucidium gnoma*
	Long-eared owl	*Asio otus*
	Short-eared owl	*Asio flammeus*
Caprimulgidae	Common nighthawk	*Chordeiles minor*
Apodidae	Vaux's swift	*Chaetura vauxi*
Trochilidae	Calliope hummingbird	*Stellula calliope*
	Rufous hummingbird	*Selasphorus rufus*
Alcedinidae	Belted kingfisher	*Ceryle alcyon*
Picidae	Red-naped sapsucker	*Sphyrapicus nuchalis*
	Downy woodpecker	*Picoides pubescens*
	Hairy woodpecker	*Picoides villosus*
	American three-toed woodpecker	*Picoides dorsalis*
	Northern flicker	*Colaptes auratus*
	Pileated woodpecker	*Dryocopus pileatus*

Appendix Families and common and scientific names for the 164 bird species detected in Nez Perce National Historical Park and Big Hole National Battlefield in 1999 (continued).

Family Name	Common Name	Scientific Name
Tyrannidae	Olive-sided flycatcher	*Contopus cooperi*
	Western wood-pewee	*Contopus sordidulus*
	Willow flycatcher	*Empidonax traillii*
	Hammond's flycatcher	*Empidonax hammondii*
	Dusky flycatcher	*Empidonax oberholseri*
	Cordilleran flycatcher	*Empidonax occidentalis*
	Say's phoebe	*Sayornis saya*
	Western kingbird	*Tyrannus verticalis*
	Eastern kingbird	*Tyrannus tyrannus*
Vireonidae	Cassin's vireo	*Vireo cassinii*
	Warbling vireo	*Vireo gilvus*
	Red-eyed vireo	*Vireo olivaceus*
Corvidae	Gray jay	*Perisoreus canadensis*
	Steller's jay	*Cyanocitta stelleri*
	Clark's nutcracker	*Nucifraga columbiana*
	Black-billed magpie	*Pica hudsonia*
	American crow	*Corvus brachyrhynchos*
	Common raven	*Corvus corax*
Alaudidae	Horned lark	*Eremophila alpestris*
Hirundinidae	Tree swallow	*Tachycineta bicolor*
	Violet-green swallow	*Tachycineta thalassina*
	Northern rough-winged swallow	*Stelgidopteryx serripennis*
	Cliff swallow	*Petrochelidon pyrrhonota*
	Barn swallow	*Hirundo rustica*
Paridae	Black-capped chickadee	*Poecile atricapillus*
	Mountain chickadee	*Poecile gambeli*
	Chestnut-backed chickadee	*Poecile rufescens*
Sittidae	Red-breasted nuthatch	*Sitta canadensis*
Certhiidae	Brown creeper	*Certhia americana*
Troglodytidae	Rock wren	*Salpinctes obsoletus*
	Canyon wren	*Catherpes mexicanus*
	Bewick's wren	*Thryomanes bewickii*
	House wren	*Troglodytes aedon*
	Winter wren	*Troglodytes troglodytes*
Cinclidae	American dipper	*Cinclus mexicanus*
Regulidae	Golden-crowned kinglet	*Regulus satrapa*
	Ruby-crowned kinglet	*Regulus calendula*
Turdidae	Western bluebird	*Sialia mexicana*
	Mountain bluebird	*Sialia currucoides*

Appendix Families and common and scientific names for the 164 bird species detected in Nez Perce National Historical Park and Big Hole National Battlefield in 1999 (continued).

Family Name	Common Name	Scientific Name
	Townsend's solitaire	*Myadestes townsendi*
	Veery	*Catharus fuscescens*
	Swainson's thrush	*Catharus ustulatus*
	Hermit thrush	*Catharus guttatus*
	American robin	*Turdus migratorius*
	Varied thrush	*Ixoreus naevius*
Mimidae	Gray catbird	*Dumetella carolinensis*
Sturnidae	European starling	*Sturnus vulgaris*
Motacillidae	Sprague's pipit	*Anthus spragueii*
Bombycillidae	Cedar waxwing	*Bombycilla cedrorum*
Parulidae	Nashville warbler	*Vermivora ruficapilla*
	Yellow warbler	*Dendroica petechia*
	Yellow-rumped warbler	*Dendroica coronata*
	Townsend's warbler	*Dendroica townsendi*
	Northern waterthrush	*Seiurus noveboracensis*
	MacGillivray's warbler	*Oporornis tolmiei*
	Common yellowthroat	*Geothlypis trichas*
	Wilson's warbler	*Wilsonia pusilla*
	Yellow-breasted chat	*Icteria virens*
Thraupidae	Western tanager	*Piranga ludoviciana*
Emberizidae	Spotted towhee	*Pipilo maculatus*
	American tree sparrow	*Spizella arborea*
	Chipping sparrow	*Spizella passerina*
	Clay-colored sparrow	*Spizella pallida*
	Brewer's sparrow	*Spizella breweri*
	Vesper sparrow	*Pooecetes gramineus*
	Savannah sparrow	*Passerculus sandwichensis*
	Grasshopper sparrow	*Ammodramus savannarum*
	Baird's sparrow	*Ammodramus bairdii*
	Fox sparrow	*Passerella iliaca*
	Song sparrow	*Melospiza melodia*
	Lincoln's sparrow	*Melospiza lincolnii*
	White-crowned sparrow	*Zonotrichia leucophrys*
	Dark-eyed junco	*Junco hyemalis*
Cardinalidae	Black-headed grosbeak	*Pheucticus melanocephalus*
	Lazuli bunting	*Passerina amoena*
Icteridae	Red-winged blackbird	*Agelaius phoeniceus*
	Western meadowlark	*Sturnella neglecta*
	Yellow-headed blackbird	*Xanthocephalus xanthocephalus*

Appendix Families and common and scientific names for the 164 bird species detected in Nez Perce National Historical Park and Big Hole National Battlefield in 1999 (continued).

Family Name	Common Name	Scientific Name
	Brewer's blackbird	*Euphagus cyanocephalus*
	Brown-headed cowbird	*Molothrus ater*
	Bullock's oriole	*Icterus bullockii*
Fringillidae	Gray-crowned rosy-finch	*Leucosticte tephrocotis*
	Cassin's finch	*Carpodacus cassinii*
	House finch	*Carpodacus mexicanus*
	Red crossbill	*Loxia curvirostra*
	Common redpoll	*Carduelis flammea*
	Pine siskin	*Carduelis pinus*
	American goldfinch	*Carduelis tristis*
	Evening grosbeak	*Coccothraustes vespertinus*

NPS 100155, August 2009